PAUL BUNYAN:
HOW A TERRIBLE TIMBER FELLER
BECAME A LEGEND

PAUL BUNYAN:
HOW A TERRIBLE TIMBER FELLER
BECAME A LEGEND

—

D. LAURENCE ROGERS

Michigan Historical Collections, Bentley Historical Library, The University of Michigan

Timber fellers in action with broad axes in Michigan's North Woods during the lumbering heyday, 1865-1885.

HISTORICAL PRESS

120 AuSable Street

Bay City, MI 48706

NOTICE REGARDING USE OF COPYRIGHTED MATERIAL

Additional copies of this book may be ordered through bookstores or by sending $19.95 plus $3.50 for postage and handling to:
Publishers Distribution Service
6893 Sullivan Road
Grawn, MI • 49637
1 (800) 345-0096

First published in the United States in 1993 by Historical Press, Inc.,
120 AuSable Street, Bay City, MI 48706.

Copyright ©1993 by D. Laurence Rogers

Publisher's Cataloging-in-Publication Data

Rogers, D. Laurence.
 Paul Bunyan: how a terrible timber feller became a legend / D. Laurence Rogers. -- 1st ed. --
Bay City, MI : Historical Press, c1993

 p. : ill. ; cm.

 Includes bibliographical references and index.
 ISBN: 0-9635369-0-7

 1. Fournier, Fabian Joe. 2. Bunyan, Paul (Legendary character) 3. Loggers--United States--Folklore. 4. Loggers--Michigan--Biography. I. Title.

SD537.52.F
634.98'092 dc20   90•84346

Manufactured in the United States of America

10 9 8 7 6 5 4 3 2 1

Book Design by Brett Radlicki, In-House Design

This book is dedicated to my mother, Annette LaFramboise Smith.
She would have loved this stuff.

Contents

Cover:

An un-assuming French Canadian farm boy, young Fabian Joseph Fournier, is photographed upon arriving in Michigan from Quebec about 1865, ready to cut timber and unwittingly become the greatest figure in American folklore.

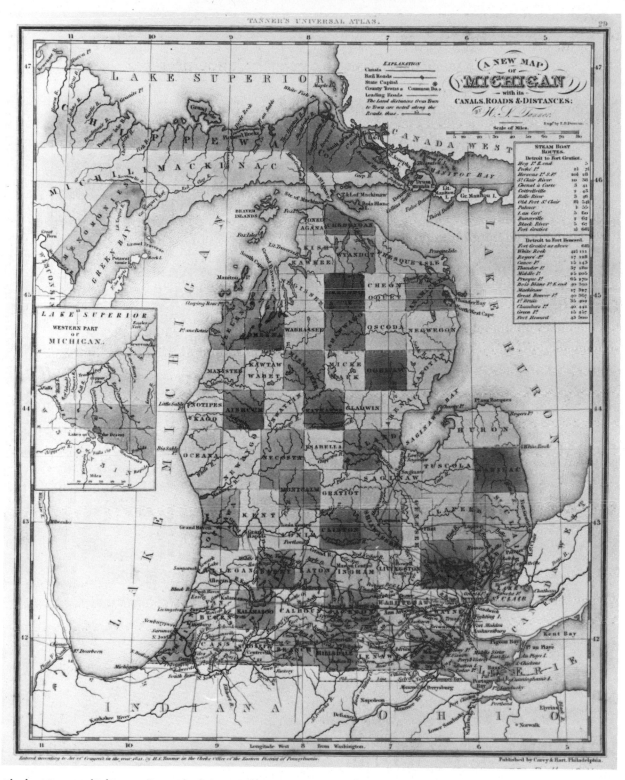

Clarke Historical Library, Central Michigan University

As lumbering began in the early 1840s, Tanner's Universal Atlas showed counties with Indian names and evolving political boundaries.

ILLUSTRATIONS

Preface

"BUNYAN, PAUL- a mythical hero of the American lumber camps for whom there is no known prototype."

So says one encyclopedia. Was this guy made up out of thin air? I wondered, guessing the encyclopedia might be wrong. Then I heard about a timber boss from the same lumbering area of Michigan where a wandering storyteller popularized the exploits of one Paul Bunyan. The trail led to a newspaperman who wrote the first story about the legendary woodsman to authors who further embellished the tales. The Bunyan legend incorporates the exploits of many men, but one man fits him best - the timber boss, Fabian "Joe" Fournier.

I first read about Fournier in 1970 while researching The Lumberman's Gazette. I soon found that some academic experts who insist that folklore must be strictly oral tales apparently were prejudiced against Paul Bunyan because the legends appeared in newspaper and magazine articles and had been exaggerated by book authors and in advertising for a lumber company. Perhaps the folklorists followed the common public misconception that lumberjacks were to blame for cutting down most of the forests. However, it was the lumber barons, with their "cut and get out" philosophy, who left Michigan little more than stump land. Timber fellers didn't make the rules of profiteering.

And here's another issue: Is it fair that gun-toting, horseback-riding cowpokes are lionized in popular history while lumberjacks, who worked on foot using only hand tools, and were never armed are often vilified for despoiling the forests? This book combats this imbalance and literary negligence and proves that Paul Bunyan was neither a myth nor a comic figure. Any self-respecting historian would certainly support such an effort.

The trail from Fournier to Bunyan grew hot when the late Harry B. Smith of Bay City, a prodigious collector of lumbering artifacts, loaned me the old tintype of Fournier that is reprinted in this book. Smith led me to Wilfrid Talbot, a former commercial fisherman who lived on Saginaw Bay. Talbot provided much of the background connecting Fournier with the Paul Bunyan legend, most notably the "Bon Jean" theory of the derivation of the name. I consider Talbot, the "ole feller" mentioned in the book, a real authority because his father, Frank, worked in the camps with Fournier. Fournier also married one of the Talbot clan. Talbot mused one day: "If only Fournier and Knute Rockne could have gotten together, (Fournier) would have been one of the greatest football players of all time." Ironically, as a timber feller Fournier as Bunyan became better known than the greatest gridiron heroes.

Mary Jane Hennigar, an enthusiastic local historian in Oscoda, Michigan, gave me a copy of the first Paul Bunyan story, written by James H. MacGillivray. Hennigar documented MacGillivray's authorship of the first Bunyan tales in an article in the Journal of Forest History, October, 1986. Ronald K. "Mac" MacGillivray, chief planner in Bay City for many years, a nephew of the author, provided vital background about his uncle James. "Mac" gave me an introduction to his cousins, the daughters of James MacGillivray (Jean Barton, of Danville, California, and Amanda Tripp, of Hollywood, Maryland), who graciously allowed me to reprint his original works on Paul Bunyan.

Some insights into the relationships between lumberjacks and lumber barons and townsfolk and immigrants come from Jeremy W. Kilar of Midland, a Delta

College history professor, author of several important books on lumbering in the Saginaw Valley and Michigan.

The late Catherine Baker, co-owner of a Saginaw River boatyard and a longtime researcher for the Bay County Historical Museum, helped in finding the location of Bay View, a long-forgotten resort on Saginaw Bay. Donald Comtois of the Saginaw River Marine Historical Society researched the history of the steamer which figured in the fateful trip to Bay View leading up to the 1875 murder of Fournier.

I searched with the late John Morrill of Grayling Michigan, a newspaper circulator with a well-developed news sense and a love of history, for Fournier's jawbone in a vain but entertaining series of local tours and we pursued the Fournier-Bunyan connection for many years.

Barbara Dinauer of Superior Abstract Co., discovered that the Morin House, where Fournier and his family lived, had become a hardware store, still standing in the old village of Banks.

Tom Fallon, my editor in the daily newspaper business, offered advice and insight as he always has and the most important ingredient-inspiration. Fellow authors Dave Miller and Dr. John Way gave me inside information about the caprices of publishing. Ty Knoy and Ellen Goldlust helped with copy editing and proofreading.

Dolores Barron Rogers helped substantially in researching the book, discovering several key elements in research libraries, as well as providing the encouragement necessary to complete the work. Others, especially Anne Hachtel, James W. Baker, Art and Joanne Nixon, Sue and Don David, Ralph Potter, Allan Blomshield, Ken Eckmyre, Emmons Miller, Stuart Gross, Wally and Lois Town and graphic artist Brett Radlicki, have taken an interest in the work.

Much is owed to the late Professor W. Cameron Meyers, my advisor in the School of Journalism at Michigan State University, East Lansing. His dedicated instruction in research methods has served me well.

Tracking down the story was time-consuming (as with many pursuits of historical facts and perspective), and difficult to complete. It took eighty years for James H. MacGillivray to receive credit for writing the first Paul Bunyan story. Fournier has been dead 117 years. The trail of the tales was there-waiting to be retraced in a book.

Incredibly, the handwritten transcript of Blinky Robertson's trial in the old Bay County Courthouse for Fournier's murder still exists. Former County Clerk Steve Toth took me to the ninth floor of the Bay County Building, moved aside a few boxes, blew away the dust of a century, and there it was - a history researcher's dream find.

It's taken more than twenty-two years, but at last the story of Fabian 'Joe' Fournier is connected to the Bunyan legend; no doubt he was the main Bunyan model as the tales developed. The theory that Paul Bunyan was indeed a real man awaits the judgment of history.

D. Laurence Rogers

Bay City, Michigan, January, 1990

revised, September, 1992

INTRODUCTION

The image of burly lumberjacks hacking down forests to put money their own pockets has been just as twisted as Hollywood's myth of the fast-drawing cowpoke "settling" the West with the six-gun.

Paul Bunyan's axe-wielding proteges didn't set out to destroy the nation's forests. They were exploited migrant workers. Lumber barons, whose motto was "cut and get out," gained most of the profit from the lumberjacks' labor. Some lumber barons also were owners of the saloons, hotels, vice resorts and gambling dens in river towns. It was there the laborers were robbed as they were blowing off steam after spring log drives. Drunken revelers were relieved of their "rolls" with the connivance of saloon keepers, gamblers, "pretty waiter girls," bouncers and cohorts. Townsfolk, especially police, were guilty of allowing this frontier version of man's inhumanity to man. This book attempts to vindicate Paul Bunyan as well as the misunderstood timber fellers. They were victims, not aggressors, as the Pine Tree Frontier was settled.

Paul Bunyan gained popularity because the timber fellers needed a symbol of strength, a larger-than-life hero to help them cope with their cruel world. This book traces how Bunyan grew to literary prominence and legendary status. The stormy, tragic life of timber feller Fabian "Joe" Fournier is linked to Bunyan. A timber boss who harvests heroic amounts of timber for his employers, Fournier engaged in the brawling, alcoholic binges commonplace among the timber fellers. He was murdered in a treacherous attack following a brawl. His killer was freed in a trial by a jury swayed by friends of the killer. Fournier was an immigrant, and his class of newcomers was used as strikebreakers in the lumber mills and was disliked by local townsfolk. The regular mill workers, mainly Anglo-Saxon descendants of early settlers, resented the French Canadian newcomers and later their Southeast European and Scandinavian counterparts.

Besides a lifetime of hard work at low wages, immigrants like Fournier often faced injury or death by accident or violence. They also faced prejudice and injustice, not incommon in early America.

Return with us now to those violent days of yesteryear when the Northwest was heavily forested. Where farmers had once burned trees to make room for crops, timber entrepreneurs invaded. Railroad companies and land speculators had moved in first, took what they needed and sold the rest for timber at about $1.25 an acre.

Intrepid timber cruisers armed only with surveying tools scoured the vast, heavily forested northern regions of Maine, Michigan, Wisconsin, Minnesota, and points West. Trudging hundreds of miles, burdened by pack and equipment, they sought the coveted prize - an unclaimed forest of virgin pine.

Entrepreneurs intrigued by the lure of "green gold" risked fortunes on a very uncertain bet, but one with a bonanza payoff. Their gamble? Finding fearless men to travel afoot to remote regions to extract timber from the frozen woods using hand tools and a few horses or oxen. In the spring timber beasts became river hogs, driving logs down fast-flowing rivers to boom companies and mills.

Penny-pinching investors hired hard-driving lumber camp bosses to get the valuable pine quickly off leased acreage. Crude log shanties were thrown up for shelter from rain and snow with only an open fireplace, the camboose, for heat. The shanty boys slept on "shotgun" bunks of logs, boards, pine boughs and straw. The

From the Collections of the Michigan State Archives, Department of State

The lone woman joining shanty boys posing at a Michigan north woods lumber camp was probably the wife of the camp boss, visiting on a Sunday. Her husband is no doubt the nattily-dressed gentleman to her left and the young boy perched on logs, left rear, their son. This group of two dozen timber fellers have cant hooks at the ready while horses are hitched and set to haul logs to banking grounds.

boss cook and his flunkies whipped up heavy grub noted for its quantity if not taste - flapjacks, sinkers (doughnuts) corn mush, beans, red horse (corned beef), sow belly (salt pork), and pie washed down with strong tea or coffee. Hunters braved wolves and bear to shoot deer for a venison stew treat. Lumber camps were no model for Emily Post; timber fellers ate with jacknives and fingers and wiped greasy hands on their shirts and pants.

Timber fellers bundled in long johns, McMillen's Canadian greys (wool pants), mackinaws and wool caps emerged from rustic camps in the murky predawn six days a week. Men groped to cutting areas at first light in seven man gangs, comprised generally of two fellers, a butter, two buckers and two skidders with a team. They chopped and sawed and hauled, with one hundred logs a daily goal, pausing only briefly to gulp beans, sourdough bread, and coffee brought to them for the midday meal. The work day lasted from dawn to dusk, at least twelve hours.

Booze was outlawed in camp, although some men dosed themselves suspiciously often with "patent medicine." Talking at meals wasn't tolerated and shirkers or dalliers were quickly handed their pay and told to hit the trail. The code was simple - shut up, get into the woods and work hard and fast. Long hours of brutal labor brought low wages, which, however, were better than the alternative - nothing. Danger lurked everywhere, perils ranging from wolves and falling trees to tricky logjams on the river.

Crews were pressed to meet demands for more and more timber for mills. Mills ran overtime to turn out posts, boards and shingles for homes, offices, and stores. Timber markets were driven by Western settlement after the Civil War, especially following the Great Chicago Fire of 1871. During that summer, the driest in history, fires destroyed entire towns throughout the Great Lakes region along with Chicago.

When lumbering began in earnest in the 1840s, Michigan was covered with 18 million acres of virgin forests, mostly white pine (Pinus Strobus). The most important timber tree of the North American continent and one of the largest, white pines reached a height of 175 feet and a butt diameter of nearly six feet at an age of 300 years. An acre of trees yielded up to 6,000 board feet of lumber. As cutting increased, concerns arose about timber resources. A great debate about clear cutting raged among timbermen. Spurred by The Lumberman's Gazette of Bay City, the press spread fears the forests were disappearing. Lumber barons, led by Arthur Hill of Saginaw, said "don't worry, there will always be trees to cut in Michigan." The optimists didn't figure on the rate timber was being cut or on the ingenuity of railroaders. Beginning in 1878, rail lines snaked through swamps to haul logs from remote timber stands. Soon little timber of value was left standing and to keep mills going logs had to be towed in huge rafts across the lakes from Canada. When Queen Victoria decreed in 1898 "all logs cut on crown lands must be manufactured within Canada," in retaliation for an 1897 U.S. import duty on white pine lumber, American mills soon went out of business.

But the gambles of investors in timber had paid off. Michigan's majestic trees were "green gold," the $4 billion lumbering bonanza over-shadowing the California Gold Rush which garnered $3 billion during the same years, 1848-98. The lumber barons' towering turreted mansions still stir awe among visitors to river towns such as Saginaw, Bay City, and Muskegon. Historian Jeremy Kilar of Delta College points out that lumber barons like Arthur Hill and Ezra Rust in Saginaw and Muskegon's Charles Hackley reinvested and left their communities with new industries while Bay City's barons took their profits and left. Bay City's millionaires were personified by Henry Sage, who never lived in the town, was accused of being

From the Collections of the Michigan State Archives, Department of State

Sawyers wield crosscuts and a feller works solo to cut huge virgin white pine. Skidder, left, waits with horse team and travois sled or "go devil" to haul logs to banking grounds, making up to ten trips to the landing from sunup to nightfall. Daily goal for each crew was an average of one hundred logs, usually sixteen footers. The light weight of pine made it possible to float the logs on rivers to the mills.

a slumlord and, after disputes over property tax increases, reluctantly fulfilled a promise to build a library for the townsfolk. However, he was the only lumber baron who left anything at all to Bay City.

While lumber barons lived in mansions, timber fellers who made them rich lived in log huts and on river rafts. The shanty boys frittered away their wages and most died penniless. Their lot was hard, dangerous work in remote camps and more exploitation when they hit town. The proverbial "company store" followed them everywhere.

Lumber barons and investors, not the timber fellers, adopted the watchword "cut and get out," abandoning land to erosion when they finished. The common woodsmen weren't swaggering timber bandits, destroying the environmental heritage of the nation, as some modern portrayers would have us believe. Instead they were primarily steady workmen slaving with hand tools. They often worked in bad weather and braved many hazards seventy to eighty hours a week. Most timber fellers were unmarried, homeless, itinerant, migrant workers. Long winters of hard, dangerous work for about a dollar a day was the lot of an ordinary "timber beast" as they were aptly called. After five or six months in the woods and dangerous, wet river drives, they lived in hotels or boarding houses, catching on as millhands, drovers, carpenters or dock wollopers, also at low wages.

In the spring, after the log drive to the booming grounds, timber fellers and river hogs feeling rich with a few hundred dollars naturally cut loose. In the river towns they were lured into squalid saloons and gambling dens. The "pretty waiter girls," saloonkeepers, and gamblers took back the cash just earned by the timber fellers. Thieves were unusually successful, especially since many of the victims were too drunk to know the difference. However, some were drugged, sandbagged from upper stories, beaten by barroom henchmen, or cheated of their "roll" in crooked card games. It was an unending ritual of self-defeat for the pitiful timber beasts and an evil but profitable ritual for the town predators.

By political design, the police kept away during the process of wholesale robbery. In Bay City, one lumber-era sheriff even owned a saloon himself. The lumbering era thus ranks high among examples of exploitation of working classes throughout history. It wasn't until the late 1880s that right-minded citizens of river towns mounted drives for law and order and hired barnstorming preachers to promote temperance. By then the lumber boom was slowing and a new industrial economy based on manufacturing was replacing the Pine Tree Frontier.

This book aims to show how the legend of Paul Bunyan was based on the real experiences of timber fellers, personified by one Fabian "Joe" Fournier, and grew through storytelling in the lumber camps. The timber fellers created Paul Bunyan, combining ancient legend and imaginative musings with reality to produce a psychic father.

Why did timbermen need Paul Bunyan? To relieve the drudgery and tension of long months of hard work in isolated camps. Stories about Bunyan helped them spiritually to transcend daily ordeals and provided inspiration to accept a dismal fate as lifelong wage slaves.

Enterprising fiction writers capitalized on the workingman's demand for a hero. Building on oral history about Paul Bunyan that had been circulating among woodsmen for years, the writers not only put the tales in print but also created more fantastic exploits.

Despite all the later claims to the contrary, Michigan was the wellspring of the Paul Bunyan legend. Perhaps initiated by one of the many French Canadian

Michigan Historical Collections, Bentley Historical Library, The University of Michigan

Buckers divide a huge felled white pine into sixteen foot logs. One of the straightest, tallest trees in the northeastern U.S., white pine average eighty to 120 feet tall with diameters of three to four feet. Early loggers reported trees 150 to 200 feet tall with diameters of five to seven feet.

immigrants in the logging camps, the legendary aspects of Paul Bunyan were fulfilled in real life by a real logger, Fournier, and others like him. There also was a preternatural basis in Saginaw Country for tales of a human of prodigious size like Bunyan. Such creatures actually existed! Inside Indian burial mounds huge skeletons of a prehistoric race of people were found by pioneers. Reports of the mysterious giant mound-builders were published in early histories of the region. A well-known Chippewa (Ojibwa) chief, David Shoppenagons, from Saginaw who lived mostly in the Grayling area, told campfire tales of a huge Indian with a prodigious appetite, much like Bunyan. Shoppenagons was a guide for the state's first conservation officer, Rube Babbitt, who told Paul Bunyan tales throughout the north country. The Bunyan tales followed the Chippewa Indian tradition of art-soo-kay, the telling of tall tales, made up mostly as the teller goes on half the night.

Michigan newspaperman James H. MacGillivray first shaped the oral tales about Paul Bunyan he had heard as a boy in the lumber camps into a story in the Oscoda, Michigan, weekly newspaper in 1906. A hodgepodge of woods lore, fact, and fiction, created an appealing literary stew. A timber "jobber" named Jimmy Conn later was reported by MacGillivray to be the main storyteller who spread the tales in the Oscoda area and later in Minnesota. MacGillivray reworked and embellished the Bunyan tales for the Detroit News-Tribune in 1910. A poem co-authored by MacGillivray and Douglas Malloch appeared in a lumbering journal in 1914, spreading the tale nationally. An artistic advertising director, William B. Laughead, adopted Paul Bunyan and gave him a visual identity through mass mailings marketing the Red River Lumber Co. of Minnesota and California. Esther Shephard and lumberjack-turned-author James Stevens in the 1920s began the incredible skein of Bunyanesque writings. H. L. Mencken, a leading literary figure

Bay County Historical Society

Chief David Shoppenagons, in Chippewa garb, poles an AuSable River canoe as conservation officer Rube Babbitt, seated with rifle at the ready, hunts deer along the banks of the AuSable. Note huge stumps on river bank, background, remaining after lumbering activity. Shoppenagons was the most noted of Northern Michigan's Native American guides.

who had encouraged many authors through the Knopf publishing empire, was the main sponsor of the Bunyan legend. He masterminded Stevens's writings on Bunyan in the Americon Mercury magazine and in books. Bunyan was so popular the tales scaled new promotional heights, related works including operas, musical scores, and epic poems by leading literary and musical figures including Robert Frost, Carl Sandburg, and W. H. Auden. Paul Bunyan captivated the world of arts and letters and the public imagination.

In search of the origin of the legend, Stevens and his wife spent nearly a year in Detroit, Bay City and Grayling. The title of his 1931 book, The Saginaw Paul Bunyan, proclaimed his conclusion. During ten months in Bay City, Stevens interviewed old-timers who related stories of lumberjacks in that area. His memory dimmed in later years, Stevens mistakenly thought he had made up Joe Fournier, the lumberjack whose exploits were so noteworthy he was famed as the "Iron Man of the Saginaw." Fournier was real but his exploits had the legendary qualities of imaginary figures.

World War II strengthened Paul Bunyan as the hero of American workingmen. Overseas, the tales grew in popularity among the military, trapped in oppressive camps and foxholes much as the timber fellers had been woods-bound work slaves. The same need for a transcendental symbol arose from the battlefields as had sprung from the travails of the Pine Tree Frontier. Servicemen alone bought 140,000 of the Bunyan books by Stevens.

As hand labor has declined, so Americans have ceased to relate to Paul Bunyan. Paul's image has been tarnished as he became a cartoon character, was called a fake, and was judged guilty by association in the destruction of the forests.

Let's take a new look at Paul Bunyan and why his legend grew and then faded.

Maybe if we understand him better, he'll make a comeback as the hero of America. Poetic justice will be served when this heroic migrant worker, the French-Canadian Paul Bunyan, as tragically portrayed in real life by Fabian Joe Fournier, is finally returned to rightful status as the legendary hero of the American ethnic melting pot.

Chapter 1
THE OLE' FELLER RECOLLECTS
HOW JOE FOURNIER BECAME PAUL BUNYAN

Ever think Paul Bunyan may have been a real, living man-not just a fictional character? Some academic skeptics contend that he was a hoax and ignore him as part of our national folklore. We don't agree with those so-called experts. Here's our side of the story, so you can judge for yourself about Joe and how he became the model for Paul.

There was a timber hewer and logging camp boss whose real life exploits mirrored early Paul Bunyan tales. Fabian "Joe" Fournier was the tough timber boss whose fame grew into fantastic stories.

Nobody ever heard of a lumberjack in those days. The timber hewers were called "fellers," because that's what they did: fell trees. Maine, Minnesota, Wisconsin, and even California claim Paul Bunyan, but Michigan, where he won fame, was his real home. Joe Fournier was born in Quebec, Canada, about 1845, and lived in the village of Bangor, or Banks, now part of Bay City, Michigan, with upriver Saginaw then the world's busiest lumber area and headquarters of Saginaw pine country.

Fournier's fame was forged by his exploits as he ranged the northern Michigan woods, in Saginaw River pine country and in the AuSable River region, from about 1865 to 1875.

Fournier, also called "Saginaw Joe," was the foreman, the boss logger, the big feller in the woods. The foreman cruised the property to pick the woods for the next day's cutting. Often he would be planning for the following day's work while the rest of the fellers had been in bed for hours. Then he'd be the first on his feet, sometimes at four o'clock in the blackness and chill of the morning. Then he'd try to be everywhere at the same time, keeping an eye on everything. He called the tune and if it wasn't right he'd have to answer to the camp owner.

Joe came to Michigan from Quebec after the Civil War when President Andrew Johnson opened up the state at a buck and a quarter an acre. Things weren't so good in Quebec, with the best jobs paying only about four dollars a month from the local "notaire," a kind of a boss clerk who worked for the landowner. Down in Saginaw country, timber hewers received a dollar a day, more than six times as much as they could earn in Quebec.

The smaller French Canadians became voyageurs, paddling canoes and helping fur-trading companies get richer. Some liked being coureurs de bois (wood runners), free-lance traders and trappers. Many struck up friendships with Indians who helped them trap beaver. The big, strong French Canadians like Joe, became timber hewers in the winter and worked in the mills, on the docks, or in the shipyards in the summer.

Joe was big enough, all right, standin' near six feet tall and weighin' 180 pounds, but he sure wasn't the giant in those tall stories they came out with later. The story tellers got crazy in the head - had him at twelve or thirteen feet tall and

From the Collections of the Michigan State Archives, Department of State

River hogs ride the logs on a fast-flowing stream using peavies for balance in this rare action shot during the dangerous drive to the mills in the spring. Floating cook shacks, called wanigans, accompanied the crews for meals on the river so little time would be lost on the drive.

888 pounds. Talk about tall stories! Most folks in Joe's times averaged only a little over five feet high, so they did all look up to him. But not that far up!

Joe was sort of good looking for the mean cuss he was. He had a broad face, strong chin, wide-set eyes, and curly hair, but no beard or moustache as the drawings in the Paul Bunyan books always show.

Though uneducated, Joe was brilliant; a camp boss needed to be smart as well as tough to control a crew of maverick timber-fellers.

Some things about Joe were almost unnatural. Even other loggers marveled at the size of his hands, half again larger than most men's with thumbs as long as the average fingers. Those huge meat hooks could handle an axe like a matchstick. Strangest of all, but absolutely true, Joe had a double row of teeth. Two complete sets, uppers and lowers - cuspids, bicuspids and molars, as a dentist would say. No logger was better equipped to chaw on stringy salt pork or bite hunks from wooden bar rails. More on that weird habit Joe was noted for later.

Joe had sloping shoulders that fooled people about his strength, which some say was equal to three or four ordinary men. He was double-jointed, which made him very agile. Joe at age nine could climb the frame of a barn and catch a squirrel, or so they said.

That kind of speed and strength paid off for a boss logger in the North Woods, where danger awaited. You know what a widow-maker is? That's when an 80, or 100 foot-high white pine comes down the wrong way and clunks a logger on the head, making his wife-if he has one-a widow. Peril to life and limb lurked on the icy roads with a horse-drawn team and a shifting skid of sixteen footers on the travois. Many a river hog's luck ran out in treacherous jams on fast-flowing spring streams. One river driver called for a double-bit axe and took his pal's leg off at the knee to get him out of a jam. Saved his life, though. Other river hogs weren't so "lucky" and their bodies, swallowed by the icy current, were never found. The run to the booming ground kept the drivers hopping on a river solid with logs from bank to bank. The rafting for the trip to the mill was easy.

When Joe first got to Saginaw Country he was the top feller in the woods. He could handle a double-bit axe or his end of a crosscut saw and, as the loggers used to say, make the pines whimper. When Joe was on the team of fellers the "timber-r-r-r-rs" echoed as fast as though two or three teams were working. He could flip logs with a peavey and find the key log in a tangle on the river to free a jam faster than any other river hog. Good timber was never splintered with dynamite when Joe was on the drive. He also was a topnotch cruiser who could spot and lay out a stand of uppers real quick. And his gangs of fellers, butters, buckers, and skidders always got their hundred logs each day. He made sure it was a full day-dawn to dusk.

Joe was tough on the camp rules: "No fighting on the river; no drinking on the river; and to bed at nine o'clock." But he freely joined in when the shanty boys were on the deacon's seat, with the camboose roarin' and the dulcey twangin', for a song or two. Nobody ever got him to tie on the hanky, but Joe would jog right in there with 'em all. Yup, the shanty boys liked ole' Joe, and worked hard for him. He sure was worth his seventy-five greenbacks a month.

The name Bunyan came from a French Canadian hero of the 1837 Papineau Rebellion, "Bon Jean," whom loggers had admired for years. "Bon Jean" means "Good John" or "Brave John," is pronounced in French something like "Bone yaahn," The name first was used by writers as Bonion then Bunyon and finally,

From the Collections of the Michigan State Archives, Department of State

Skidders drag load of sixteen-footers out of the woods with teams pulling a travois, or "go devil," to the banking grounds to be decked in readiness for the spring drive. Dangers in lumbering operations such as this were shown by the fact that forty-five shanty boys perished in accidents during one cutting season in Michigan's north woods.

Bunyan. Loggers often called a strong, tough woodsman a "Bon Jean." By adding Paul, a common French name, our hero Joe Fournier became Paul Bunyan. We've always believed Fournier's feats were exaggerated and other exploits added to create Paul Bunyan.

When you read more I think you'll agree: this real timber feller was hewn into a real big feller-Paul Bunyan, a legend much larger than life-by storytellers and writers using their imaginations.

Fournier was a great logger-and brawler-until treachery ended his fighting days. He was murdered on the Third Street dock in Bay City the night of November 7, 1875. The villain surprised him in the dark behind his back and caved in his skull with a ship carpenter's mallet.

Strange as it may seem, that murder helped to begin one of America's greatest legends. You see, all the news about the murder and then about the trial of Blinky Robertson, who did the deed, got lots of people talking about Joe Fournier.

Tales were told of Joe's amazing strength and how he saved many of his men in tight spots in the woods and on the river. The amount of timber cut by Joe's crews seemed to grow as the stories were told and retold. Then the stories about Joe got all mixed up with other tales old timers told about the original Bon Jean, the big Frenchman who fought the Queen's troops in Canada and then headed a logging crew. Pretty soon you couldn't tell Bon Jean from Fournier.

As the years passed, it became impossible to separate the tales about Joe from those about Paul. Around thousands of campfires the tales were repeated over the years, and each storyteller added a little to the size of Paul Bunyan, the amount of timber his crews cut, and his exploits, making up most of it as they went along.

More than thirty years after Joe Fournier's murder a newspaper- man who had heard the tales as a boy in the lumber camps sat down to write the story for the first time. We'll look at the writer and how the story continued to grow later.

Chapter 2
SAGINAW COUNTRY: THE SAUK'S HAUNTED SWAMP AND BUNYAN'S STOMPING GROUND

"Interminable Swamp" was the warning written across maps of Michigan after it was surveyed by the U.S. Army in the early 1800s for land grants to war veterans. The soldier-surveyors encountered huge mosquitoes in the swampy regions, especially the Saginaw Valley, Paul Bunyan's stomping grounds. Camped at Saginaw, the army garrison suffered greatly from fever during a wet fall. The surveyors soon wanted no part of the place and warned the rest of the world to stay away, too. "Nothing but Indians, muskrats and bullfrogs could possibly exist here," the troop commander reported. Other more literary detractors described the interior of Michigan as "an impenetrable swamp, in whose slimy recesses the cowardly wolf held carnival by day and the ill-omened owl hooted away the lonely vigils of the gloomy night."

The huge swamps surrounded the Saginaw River and its network of tributaries - the Shiawassee, Cedar, Bad, Pine, Tobacco, Chippewa, Salt, Molasses, Cass, Flint and Tittabawassee - and innumerable riverine creeks and drains. This wide-ranging watery network, radiating about 50 miles to the east, west and south,

Library of Congress

Small steamer Langell Boys is loaded with pine board from a dock on the Saginaw River. Work is supervised by an official of the Saginaw firm, Mershon, Schuette, Parker and Company, which owned the steamer. In the banner year of 1888, over four billion board feet of lumber was cut in the mills of the Saginaw Valley, enough to make a sidewalk of two inch planks, four feet wide, that would reach around the earth almost four times.

constitutes the largest drainage basin in the state, comprising 6,260 square miles, three million acres, about equal to the combined area of Connecticut and Delaware. Those tributaries were used to transport the logs from the vast forests of the area to market and made Saginaw Country the greatest pine territory in the world. "Hawkers" sold Saginaw pine in Chicago, Cleveland, Buffalo and points east and some of it ended up at the far reaches of the globe. Saginaw pine was the finest, clearest, most easily worked wood available. It was so bouyant it was called "cork" pine. Besides the swamps, mosquitoes and quality of wood, Saginaw became known for other, more wondrous reasons.

Archaeologists say Saginaw was one of the earliest sites of aboriginal habitation in North America. For thousands of years, Indians lived in villages on high ground along the banks of the Saginaw and other, narrower rivers in the area.

The heavily wooded region known as Saginaw Country stretched north from the swamps of Saginaw two hundred miles to the Straits of Mackinac and east 35 miles from Lake Huron to about the center of the state on a line north and south bisecting Grayling and Otsego Lake. This was the prime hunting and fishing ground controlled by the fierce Sauk Indian tribe when the white man first arrived. Saginaw Country abounded with deer, bear, moose, elk, turkey, beaver, fisher, marten, otter and mink along with predators such as wolves, fox, bobcats, lynx, panthers and wolverine. Pioneers reported the sky would be blackened by flights of passenger pigeons, ducks, geese and swans when startled by the approach of a human. Fish ranging from huge muskellunge and sturgeon, trout, walleyed pike, black bass, whitefish, catfish, pickerel and perch thrived in Saginaw Bay and the rivery network. Indians made a game of catching fish by hand and also would chase

Annette LaFramboise Smith Collection

The statement that game abounded in Saginaw Country is borne out by this wagon laden with elk, moose and deer, all of enormous size and with huge antlers, photographed shortly after the return of a party of hunters from the north to Bay City in the 1880s. Many hunting clubs established camps of huge acreage in Saginaw Country and AuSable Country after the lumbering era and some still exist today.

fish trapped under the ice until they were exhausted and could be taken out through a hole chopped in the ice. The bay's ice was clear enough so fish could easily be seen. The Indians also were partial to the area's many salt springs.

Even before the adverse report of the swampy conditions by the soldier-surveyors, Saginaw Country was shunned for another reason. After the Sauks were massacred by other tribes about 1650, Saginaw Country was believed to be haunted.

The French explorer and colonizer of Canada, Samuel de Champlain, found the Sauks when he sought refuge from storms in Saginaw Bay in 1611. Champlain delineated the mouth of the Saginaw River in a rough drawing said to be as correct as today's maps. The area now known as Michigan became part of Champlain's "New France" in 1622. Jesuit priests Charles Raymbault and Isaac Jogues visited the site of Sault Ste. Marie as early as 1641 to convert the Indians to the Roman Catholic faith. Even as the Jesuits were proselytizing the Chippewa and Ottawa tribes to the north, other Algonquin tribes in the lower peninsula engaged in a wide-ranging feud against the Sauks who inhabited Saginaw Country. The Sauks had inflicted the greatest indignity of Indian warfare; they had captured a Chippewa brave and his squaw during a raid at Traverse Bay and brought them south as slaves to the main Sauk village at Bay City.

The Chippewa, Ottawa, and Potawatomi Indians and allied tribes drove the Sauks out of the Saginaw region they had controlled since before recorded history. The Sauks were massacred in a series of surprise raids by overwhelming numbers of the enemy. The three warring tribes, backed by Menominees and Dakotas from the west and Mohawks and tribes of the Algonquin Six Nations from the east, met in war council at Port Huron and decided to destroy the Sauks and make their lands a common hunting ground. The attackers gathered a large army at Mackinac Island and stole down the west shore of Lake Huron in bark canoes to a place called Petobegong (now Tobico Marsh State Game Area just north of Bay City). Splitting into two groups, one crossing the bay, the massed warriors attacked from the east and west against the Sauks' main village on the Saginaw River. Battles also were fought on the Tittabawassee, Shiawassee, Cass and Flint. Another attacking army was said to have approached the Sauks from Detroit, engaging in the most extensive battles on the Flint River.

According to history, only twelve Sauk females were spared and were exiled to the west. After the massacre, Indians believed the ghosts of the Sauks stalked the land. There were occasional reports of mysterious solitary Indians killing unwary travelers or of lone Sauks being spotted. An Indian chief, Ton-dog-a-ne, in 1840 told of killing a Sauk while hunting when a boy.

The Chippewa gave the country its name, calling it "O-Sauk-e-non," Land of the Sauks, which evolved to "Saguina", "Saguinam", "Sikenaw", "Sakenaw", and finally, "Saginaw". The Sauk were first mentioned in print under their Huron name Hvattoehronen, meaning "people of Saginaw." Other translations of Saginaw were "the opening", "the mouth of a river", and "place of the Sauks".

For a while Saginaw Country was believed by the other Indian tribes to be so haunted as to be uninhabitable. It was considered a penal colony and Indians who committed a crime were banished there or fled to that haunted ground. So many Sauk skulls were found on an island in the Saginaw River that it was known as "Skull Island." Many of the skeletons bore the evidence of death by violence. No wonder the Indians were afraid; the place was a huge graveyard. The Miller and Bauer families, first settlers in Frankenlust Township, Bay County, arriving by canoe up

Squaconning Creek, discovered so many human bones lying about they were forced by Christian conscience to conduct a mass burial — some 200 years after the massacre!

Other Indian graves later were found in huge mounds all over the valley. Stone axes, knives and broken pottery were found in the burial mounds. Mounds were about seven feet high and up to three acres in area. In Bay City, the mounds were located along the river, at Twenty-Second and Twenty-Fourth streets on the east side and on Linn just south of Midland Street, between Midland and Salzburg and near State and Marquette on the west side. Separate from the mounds, Indian burial grounds were found along the Saginaw, Kawkawlin, Pinconning and Saganing rivers, near the sites of old Indian villages.

Strangest of all, the skeletons of a very different race of people were unearthed at a level below that of the other graves, obviously from quite an earlier era. In excavating for the cellar of the Bay City Brewery, pioneer W. R. McCormick reported finding three skeletons of very large stature, with large earthen pots at the head of each. These giant skeletons were found at a depth of eleven feet while the others were at the four foot depth. While the first group was obviously Indian, with the skulls having high cheekbones and a receding forehead, the lower group was from a more ancient race of an entirely different formation of skull. McCormick was unable to preserve any of the skulls as they crumbled to dust soon after exposure to the air. Ancient pottery and stone which had been fired was found with these bodies. This race also was skilled in the art of working metal and apparently extracted copper by heating rock and cooling it with water. A copper awl, copper kettles and small silver canoe of exquisite workmanship, its ends tipped with gold, were found with other bones. Other similar skeletons of large humans were found in mounds on the Rifle River, in what was then known as Township Twenty-Two north. In one mound near the headwaters of the AuSable River, some sixty miles north of Bay City, curious diggers uncovered the skeleton of a man estimated to be at least seven feet tall with a skull nearly twice as large as an ordinary person's. Did the party of Indians accompanying Bay City fur trader Michael Daley which made that awesome find in the early 1800s start the legend of a huge woods-dwelling human which evolved into the character known today as Paul Bunyan? Perhaps the seeds of legend were sown when the skeleton was found because tales of huge Indians later were told by the Chippewa chief David Shoppenagons. Whether the connection between the aboriginal giants and the giant logger of Canadian origin ever was made will never be known for sure, but it is, of course, possible. It is the type of legend which could transcend the races and be part of the folklore of both cultures. If that is so, it may be confirmation the Paul Bunyan legend sprang up in Saginaw Country.

Although the Jesuits attempted to establish missions in Saginaw Country and planted fruit trees on the banks of the Saginaw River, the black-robed priests were unable to create a permanent settlement or even a trading post. The Chippewa, however, were good cultivators, especially in the fertile soil of the valley delta. The British sent from Mackinac Island to buy corn from the industrious Chippewa at Saginaw in 1779. Fur traders found a bonanza. So many furs were shipped to France that King Louis XIV, under pressure from fur merchants, ordered all French fur traders and soldiers out of Michigan.

After battling Great Britain in King William's War in Europe for eight years until 1697, Louis XIV ordered his soldiers to return to Michigan and other western areas in an effort to confine the English to the Atlantic Coast. Detroit was settled in 1701 and abandoned settlements such as Sault Ste. Marie, St. Ignace and Niles were reoccupied.

After the so-called "French and Indian Wars," mainly in the east to repel the expansion of English settlements, the Treaty of Paris in 1763 gave all of Canada and Michigan to Great Britain. The second Treaty of Paris, in 1783, supposedly gave the region to the new United States of America, an agreement which infuriated British fur traders. Because of their displeasure with the treaty, the English retained control of forts at Detroit and Michilimackinac, using Michigan as its base for the fur trade during the Revolutionary War and until Jay's Treaty (1795) was enforced in 1796. Michigan then became part of the Northwest Territory of the United States.

The Indians of the Saginaw Valley were said to be misbehaving and treacherous, but who could blame them for dissuading interlopers in their valuable hunting and fishing territory? The Indians aided the English in the War of 1812, but put up little serious opposition to the white man's gradual invasion and finally yielded their happiest hunting grounds for the paltry sum of $3,000 plus $1,000 annual payments, in 1819. Governor Lewis Cass of Michigan Territory "negotiated" the Treaty of Saginaw in two weeks by bribing the Chippewa with liquor and pronounced "fair and generous" the token payment for six million acres. The soldier-surveyors who encountered swamps and mosquitoes built a fort in 1822 at Saginaw. The native population dwindled from 5,000 to about 2,000 by 1865 when they ceded the last 40,000 acres at Bay City and moved to the Isabella reserve at Mount Pleasant and settlements at Saganing, Indiantown and Quanicassee.

The French traveler and savant Alexis de Tocqueville and companion Gustave de Beaumont, touring the U.S. in 1831, encountered the lingering phobia against Saginaw Country. An old Mohawk warrior in Buffalo, New York, whose services

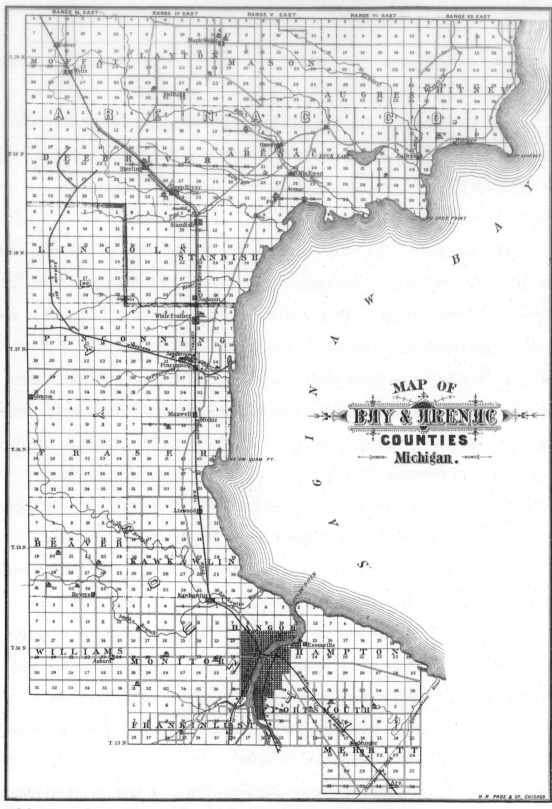

Old map shows Bay County, Saginaw Bay and rivers.

they sought as a guide, told the Frenchmen to beware of the Indians of the haunted region of O-Sauk-e-non. Pontiac innkeeper Amasa Bagley warned the pair about venturing further north: "You want to go to Saginaw! To Saginaw Bay! Two reasonable men, two well-educated foreigners want to go to Saginaw Bay! ... "Do you know that Saginaw is the last inhabited place until the Pacific Ocean; that from here to Saginaw hardly anything but wilderness and pathless solitudes are to be found?" Tocqueville viewed the Saginaw Valley far differently, describing it a "delicious, perfumed, gorgeous dwelling, a living palace made for man, though as yet, the owner had not taken possession." Tocqueville predicted: "In a few years these impenetrable forests will have fallen; the sons of civilization will break the silence of the Saginaw; the banks will be imprisoned by quays; its current, which now flows on unnoticed and tranquil through a nameless waste, will be stemmed by the prows of vessels. We were perhaps the last travelers allowed to see the primitive grandeur of this solitude."

Thus the shunned and haunted valley was proclaimed a paradise by a visiting savant. Later, Henry Wadsworth Longfellow caught the same spirit of the Saginaw in his epic poems, "Evangeline" and "The Song of Hiawatha." In 1849 the poet entertained the Ojibwa chief, Kah-ge-ga-bowh, at his home in Boston and heard tales of the beloved hunting grounds. In Longfellow's works, the Acadians, driven from their homes, find solace in the hunting lodges of the valley; Evangeline seeks her Gabriel in vain on the banks of the Saginaw. A village on the west bank of the river and a park in Bay City as well as a hotel which burned in 1975 were named after Wenona, the mother of Longfellow's Hiawatha.

Rivers rush through the valley northward into Saginaw Bay, joining Lake Huron and merging into colder Canadian waters. The bay's narrow mouth spans 26 miles

Computer Art by Mary Dolores Barron-Rogers

LaSalle's ship Griffon, beset by a fierce storm on Saginaw Bay, finally found safety in the lee of the Charity Islands. The Griffon, first sailing ship on the Great Lakes, was built by LaSalle's men in New York. Laden with furs bound for Montreal, the Griffon was lost in a storm and rumors are that the bones of the huge captain, Luke the Dane, and his four crewmen were found in a cave years later. The ship, originally sighted under water, may have slipped off the reef where it had been impaled, but no trace has ever been found.

from AuSable Point southeast to Pte. Aux Barques, its waters reaching 51 miles south to the Saginaw River in Bay City. Saginaw Bay, too, has legendary status, some mariners denouncing it as "a gulf of terror" and others calling it "the most unpredictable body of water this side of the Bay of Biscay." The bay is famed for its petulance. Short, vicious waves wrack boats with incessant thuds. Higher winds create longer, hacking waves-not the gentle rollers of the wide oceans, but nasty, snapping waves with high peaks and cavernous valleys that swallow up boats and ships, plunging mariners to a horrible death buried alive in raging waters.

The French explorer, Rene'-Robert Cavelier, Sieur de LaSalle, guided his ill-fated ship, the 45-ton, five cannon Le Griffon into the lee of the Charity Islands in 1679 fleeing the fury of a Saginaw Bay storm assaulting the craft as it rounded Point Aux Barques. "Even the stout heart of LaSalle was made to quake with fear, and he called upon all to commend themselves to heaven and promised to build a chapel in honor of St. Anthony if they should be spared," was the report. LaSalle was following Jean Nicolet, who crossed the bay by canoe 50 years before. Later that year the Griffon was lost in Lake Huron returning to Montreal from Green Bay, laden with furs bound for France, but LaSalle was not aboard.

It is fitting that such a land of danger and mystery, about which warnings had been issued for centuries, haunted by the ghosts of the Sauks and skeletons of mysterious giants, should be the wellspring of the legend of the greatest timber feller, Paul Bunyan. This storied valley rang with a tale that emerged from a murderous attack that snuffed out a titan of the woods, Fabian "Joe" Fournier. Let's go back through the mists of time to a morning in a lumber camp after that fateful night on the Third Street dock...

Chapter 3
WHY IT FELL GHOSTLY QUIET
IN THE LOGGING CAMP IN WINTER OF '75

Daylight in the swamp - and no Joe Fournier.

A hundred loggers were scratching, grunting, and squinting at four o'clock in the morning, crawling out of shotgun bunks, pulling on wool pants over wire-haired long johns, chewing on cookee's sourdough bread and washing down greasy "morning glory" flapjacks with bitter molasses and tea as strong as Boston Harbor during the Tea Party.

But there was no Joe to howl "hurry up" in this camp, and no merry morning song to put the good fellers in the mood to fall to with a will. The choppers would have to tackle the towering forest without Joe's hollering. Daylight in the swamp and no Joe Fournier.

Sawyers would be bucking trunks and Joe wouldn't have a say about "shorts." Swampers would be clearing roads alone, and skidders, loaders, and bankers would be chewing and puffing too long at the banking grounds. Scalers and stampers would likely get sloppy with their measuring and counting and marking.

The lumber camp crew had come up to the woods by train from Saginaw in September, carrying a few personal belongings in their "turkeys" slung over their

From the Collections of the Michigan State Archives, Department of State

Hungry timber fellers cast surly looks as they wait impatiently for the cookees (flunkies) to serve their "chuck." Evening supper was the "square meal" of the day, consisting mainly of beans, red horse (corned beef), sow belly (salt pork), potatoes, corn mush and sourdough bread. Flunky at left is holding what appears to be bread or pie dough. Kind-hearted boss cooks often allowed free chuck to out-of-work shanty boys wandering from camp to camp in search of a job.

shoulders. Every man on the train had a bottle and a story about their time off since last May and every ride north into the woods was a ride to remember. Every trip had its drunks and its fights and its songs, all the way to West Branch, or Roscommon or Grayling or 100 miles to Otsego Lake. Then it was afoot or by wagon to points east or west to the familiar camp. Timber fellers recalled trains arriving at northern stations with all the windows broken out from the rowdy trip.

Once in the woods, all these boys wanted to do was to cut pine. They wouldn't lay an axe to a popple or be caught dead in a bunkhouse with a popple log in it. Cutting pine was the job they had, and they were proud to say they could chop down forty or fifty 200 footers and saw them into logs every day. They'd cut their teeth on double-bit axes and cross-cut saws and that's all these shanty boys knew.

Nothing stopped fellers like this crew, Joe Fournier's crew, when they got started in the woods. It could be 20 below zero and none of them would stop to build a fire. If the bull cook came along with dinner on a bobsled and built a fire, why one of these boys might stand beside it while he ate. But he'd never take time out to build a fire himself. That's the kind of crew Joe had. They were tough!

None of these boys would ever change a shirt, either. If a shirt or pants went bad, they'd just go over to the wanigan, get a new pair and put them on and keep right on going through the season. Some of the boys had five or six shirts or pairs of pants on by the time spring rolled around. They were wearing the same underwear, too.

All that work and a dollar a day. It was a great life and you had to be some kind of a man to be part of it. Lumber camps lured different kinds of fellers, Poles, Germans, Swedes, Welshmen, Norwegians, Cornishmen, Finns, Irish, Scots, French-Canadians, Indians and a few Negroes. If the boss couldn't speak lots of languages, he was in trouble, but somehow Joe got the message across: you're

From the Collections of the Michigan State Archives, Department of State

Chow time was serious business in the lumber camps, as the grim looks from this gang of fellers indicates. Camps had a strict "no talking at meals" rule so fellers wouldn't be dallying while work awaited. This scene is at one of H. M. Loud's fourteen camps in Au Sable Country. Joe Donnelly, later a camp foreman, is at right (fourth man in from feller in foreground).

a pine chopping shanty boy for H.M. Loud and Co. and you're tough and proud.

On Saturday night in Grayling or Roscommon, these boys were known to drink what they called squirrel corn. That was whiskey so bad a man who drank it could run right up one side of a pine tree and down the other. You could work up a pretty bad dry in a lumber camp.

But it just wasn't the same in Saginaw Country in the timber cutting season of 1875-76 with Joe Fournier gone, dead as a burned over tree stump. The boys kept moving, right up to Gabriel time, but when that tocsin sounded the beans and salt pork didn't taste the same as usual. Even a syrup dessert couldn't sweeten the sour mood.

When the two dozen weary shanty boys settled in, hardly a word was heard. At the end of the long day you peeled off wet clothes and hung them in the bunkhouse and they steamed all night. You lit your pipe or took a chaw of tobacco and relaxed, played checkers, did your mending, sang a few songs or told a few stories. But nobody was singing or even talking. All anybody could think of was: "Joe's gone."

Axes were ground with no whistling. Horses were fed with nobody talking to them. Ever see a horse look at you fishy-eyed? Ol' Inkslinger in the clerk's shack got by with no kidding or joshing - the fellers just got their pay and went.

It wasn't natural. Then again, what happened to Joe wasn't natural, either. It was murder of the foulest sort.

Chapter 4
RED SASH BRIGADE ON "HELL'S HALF MILE"- WHERE JOE COMES TO AN UNTIMELY END

When the loggers tied on their scarlet sashes after the drive and went to town, it was Joe's undoing.

At its peak, Michigan's North Woods were lumbered by about 40,000 hard-muscled shanty boys and river hogs. After six or seven months of Spartan solitude among the pines, the men were ready to tip more than a few drinks, roll some dice or turn some cards, and prospect boldly for female companionship. Tying a fancy red sash around their waists to brighten up their grubby work duds to visit town was just the start for the invading timber boys. Townsfolk called the swaggering, fun-lusting bunch the "Red Sash Brigade." Together with sailors, millhands and dock-wollopers, the brigade disturbed the peace in every river town every May from the 1850s to the 1890s.

Despite the fervent condemnation of temperance groups and indignant hell fire and brimstone tent preachers like the Reverend Henry Chance, who won the moniker "Buck Eye Broad Axe," sin and crime thrived in the rustic booming grounds at the end of the drive. While the logs were sorted, graded, and assembled for sale,

Annette LaFramboise Smith Collection

Washington Avenue, looking north from Columbus, in 1870s Bay City. Tower at left is the fire department, with fire company drilling in the street in front. At right is a school also with a bell tower. At bottom left on the corner is the the small foundry which became the massive Industrial Works. Today's Romanesque City Hall was built in the 1880s and would be situated about in the center of this picture.

the timber fellers cut loose on a spree to make up for a long, lonely winter in the woods and a bone-chilling wet spring on the river.

In river towns like Muskegon, Ludington, Manistee, Cheboygan, Alpena, Bay City and Saginaw, howling river hogs blew off enough steam to drive a dozen locomotives clean to California. About five thousand loggers hit Bay City each spring, most headed for the infamous "Hell's Half Mile" and notorious inner sanctums of the "Block o' Blazes." Proper burghers and matrons wisely avoided the gaslit saloons and sin dens catering to carousing woodsmen. After all, business is business and lonely shanty boys will be thirsty, howling shanty boys at the end of the long cutting season and river drives. What timber beasts howled for came in whalebone corsets and little brown jugs - the saloon ladies and potent booze of Water Street.

While townsfolk feared the Water Street region during the spring spree, it was the timber fellers themselves who should have steered clear. The descent into the Hell of Water Street held real danger for the vulnerable timber beasts on their sprees. While female beer slingers were as predatory as their male henchmen, some were actually female impersonators — the proverbial wolves in sheeps' clothing — luring the unwary into a false promise of sexual liaison and robbing their hard-earned cash.

There was no howling in the presence of real ladies, however, because the loggers' unwritten code held that no man could offend, insult, or molest a woman; no man could speak lightly of a woman of good reputation without suffering swift, violent justice at the hands of fellow loggers. A vigilante posse in Grayling, riled about an unruly timber feller who had insulted a lady, strung him up between two Norway pines and didn't cut down his body until the next day.

Joe Fournier followed the unwritten code of the timbermen and was never known to accost a woman, although he never shrank from a fight with a man. By the code, women, children, and the helpless were always safe when woodsmen were around.

While Grayling was downright inhospitable to loggers rude to ladies, Roscommon won the reputation of hell-raising headquarters and was reputed to be the toughest town in the nation at the time. Shooting went on all night, mostly by drunks not able to get a bed on a barroom floor or even on hay in a two-bit-a-night barn. Jail was an empty boxcar that cooled off even the most fired-up timber feller when the temperature dropped to around zero. One tough guy who broke out of the boxcar was collared by the surly bantam rooster size sheriff, handcuffed to a tree, and left outside all night to sober up. Roscommon made the Wild West seem tame. A floating gang of 2,000 or so Mackinaw-clad jacks, all wildly spending money, populated Roscommon. Men with $75 in their pocket one day would be hiring out the next day because they were broke from drinking and gambling.

The infamous "Stockade" was a wooden enclosure near Clare in which a licentious saloonkeeper kept a harem of prostitutes in so-called "white slavery" for the diversion of randy lumberjacks. Roscommon had its own stockade, Jonnie Mahoney's vice resort, south of town, where the girls were guarded by fierce dogs.

The Weidemann and Wright Hotel in West Branch charged a timber feller named Jerry R. forty cents for dinner and two dollars for two quarts of bourbon whiskey and later had to charge him with trying to burn down the hotel. "Bad" Tom Hayes became the first to be buried in Brookside Cemetery in West Branch because of his thirst for whiskey. It seems a drunken Hayes wouldn't take "no" for an answer when refused a drink by the young nephew of the owner of the West Branch Hotel. Furious, Hayes dove over the bar and the feisty lad was forced to fend off the attacker with a shot to the chest from his uncle's trusty six-shooter. The boy, who even had the grace to fire a warning shot, was acquitted by a jury which ruled his action "justifiable homicide."

Ogemaw County, of which West Branch is the county seat, was typical of north woods counties in keeping the cost of law enforcement as low as possible. Much like Roscommon which used a boxcar for a jail, Ogemaw's jail was a series of iron cages after fire destroyed the jail building and courthouse.

Northern towns were much like river towns, sporting numerous saloons to fuel the thirsty shanty boys. A temperance-minded school teacher, offered a job in West Branch, declined the job because the town had too many gin mills. Roscommon had only thirty six buildings but thirty four of them were bars.

After Grayling, Roscommon, West Branch or Clare, one wonders why loggers couldn't wait to find more trouble. In the riverside mill towns shanty boys were quickly relieved of their pay if they hadn't already been fleeced by Detroit gamblers, who often infiltrated the camps. In Bay City - reputed to have the wildest saloons and gambling dens - loggers made a beeline to the Hell's Half Mile strip on Water Street. Some nasty Water Street sin dens even had trapdoors to the water through which drunken lumberjacks were dumped when their pockets were empty. The worst hellhole was the Catacombs, at Third and Water, which not only had a trapdoor but also a slide into the river for bodies. The Steamboat saloon on the Third Street Bridge approach was the main entrance to the three story sin palace, headquarters of the Catacombs district connected by underground passageways. The mysterious cave-like Catacombs were entered under the Third Street Bridge just above river level where several dives were handy for dock-wollopers, ship's crewmen and others engaged in loading lumber. Townsfolk tagged the Do Drop Inn,

Bay County Historical Society

Bay City's notorious Water Street, looking north from Sixth. Buildings at left line the riverbank. Right is the elegant, three story Fraser House, largest among the town's more than 100 hostelries, boasting one of the state's most popular gaming casinos in the wide-open lumbering days.

on Water near Center Avenue, a tough resort for good reason; many an unwary river hog spent his last vacation there. Other notorious sin dens were the Red Light, located on Fourth Street between Saginaw and Water streets; the Brunswick, on Washington between Third and Fourth; the Blood Tub, further up river at Garfield and Twelfth; Oak Hall, Fourth and Water; Ma Duffy's and the Senate on Water Street; and George Cook's on Third. So many river hogs once jammed Cook's that the floor caved in, but planks were quickly placed across the span and the carousing continued without letup.

The St. James Restaurant, in the St. James Hotel on the west side of Water between Center and Fifth, which figures in Fournier's murder, was reputed to have a hidden undergound sporting room linked to the Catacombs. Even after the city's answer to the crime wave, tough, towering policeman Nathaniel Murphy, was hired on the job in 1876 soon after the murder of Fournier and began to crack the skulls of lawbreakers, the secret room was never detected by authorities. A pugilist of some repute, one Tug McGivern, is said to have brawled with a pugnacious lumberjack in the clandestine chamber under the St. James Restaurant before a carousing crowd. The battle, which was not reported in the daily press, supposedly ended in a bloody, but gentlemen's draw, much as did the epic struggle in the Red Keg Saloon between Fournier and Silver Jack Driscoll.

Entertainment of Fournier's day was not limited to brawls between lumberjacks. Racy Vaudeville-type variety shows were enjoyed by lumberjacks in Billy Fuller's variety house, on Third between Saginaw and Water, Boardwell's Opera House and the three-story building known as the Catacombs, just across Third Street from the Wolverton Hotel, lumberjack headquarters. A selection of violent diversions also was available, including fighting bulldogs, rat-killing contests between terriers, and cock fights. All these forms of cruel and perverted "fun" were later banned by society but ran without regulation during the wide open days of Hell's Half Mile. The wildest tales of the time were of a hard - drinking Irishman, nicknamed "Paddy the Dog," who sometimes could be lured by a big enough purse and copious quantities of booze to enter the pit and kill rats or even fight bulldogs with his teeth. Paddy's horribly scarred face obviously reflected the folly of his drunken pastime.

On the outskirts of town along AuSable State Road, the old sand ridge Indian trail leading north, various sin dens were located to catch the last remaining money from timber fellers on their way back to the camps. Some of these were the "Red House," the "Sand Hill," and "Peck's." News reports during the waning years of lumbering told of one of these dens, operated by a John H. Wilkins and offering "more or less beer and 40-rod," burning while police, who had lately closed the place down, watched with obvious pleasure (40-rod was liquor said to be so strong no man could drink it and walk more than 40 rods). Gradually, as "civilization" invaded the northern woods, liquor dealers followed the trail blazed by gamblers and established similar dens catering to thirsty lumberjacks who couldn't wait for the spring spree.

There were easier ways to take the shanty boys' money. At Scotty Maguire's Alhambra, Fifth and Saginaw streets, gambling stakes ran as high as $100 on the turn of a card. The town's biggest hotel, the Fraser House, sported roulette wheels and other gaming. Horse and buggy races on Fifth and Center avenues in Bay City as well as pacers at racetracks on plank roads and in East Saginaw also attracted lots of bets. Big money was staked on rowing regattas pitting teams from Saginaw and Bay City in double sculls between the Third Street and 23rd Street bridges. Some Bay City highbinders once brought in a fast-rowing team of Frenchmen who

Annette LaFramboise Smith Collection

Gamblers operating out of a tent in the woods use a trunk for a card table. Note bottle of liquor as well as pistol close at hand, in case either is needed, and joker with card in hat. Gamblers infiltrated the lumber camps, taking jobs for a time to size up the crew, find out how much money they had and the games they might be enticed into so they could skin them of their "rolls."

had just won a regatta in England and skinned the backers of Saginaw's team on a $1,000 bet. Runners raced a mile down Center Avenue with the finish line at Water Street to provide more betting sport. Bay Cityans even bet on themselves in standing broad jump matches with visiting athletes.

The temperance preachers, first shocked in Bay City by lumberjacks and Indians reeling drunkenly from the saloons, were not able to turn the tide of sin and crime without strong police support. The preachers' efforts to urge compliance with rum laws incurred the wrath of profiteering saloonkeepers. The Rev. C.C.C. (Calvin Christopher Columbus) Chillson and his wife were targets of intimidation as they tried to spread their fervent message of temperance. Their associate, Rev. P.O. Johnson, quit his post as missionary among the Indians at Kawkawlin in futility. Chillson's home was stoned and his wife, walking down the gatepath at her home, was confronted by a man from a nearby saloon aiming a gun at her. Fearless, the minister's wife continued toward the gunman. Cowed by her bravery, the assailant turned the gun to the side and fired, the ball whizzing by her ear. Chillson, who also was a justice of the peace, was more than once assaulted by saloon rowdies and shot at by a drunken ruffian trying to discourage Chillson's anti-saloon work. It was too much for the Chillsons, who moved to the more sedate West Side where they bought a farm. Despite the valiant efforts of temperance preachers, Bay City obviously was not yet ready to exorcise the evil elements preying on lumberjacks and wouldn't be until after Fournier's murder.

Other Bay City women were on the opposite side of righteousness and were as tough and feisty as male culprits. The wife of the proprietor of the Do Drop Inn was reportedly a very flashy type who was connected with a row which ended in murder at the resort. She was convicted and sentenced to five years in prison by Judge

Sanford M. Green (also the jurist in the Fournier murder case). When asked if she had anything to say, the tough saloonkeeper's wife answered: "you might just as well make it ten years." The judge said: "it isn't too late, Madam, we will make it ten years."

Captain Augustus H. Gansser, who wrote a history of Bay County in 1905, described Hell's Half Mile:

> **"The writer was a newsboy in 1883-85, and he well recalls the riotous life among the lumbermen even at that late day. Prize fights were the daily attraction at some of the Third Street resorts. Gaudy women catered to the thirsty in other resorts, or sang and danced on rough board stages, while below them on rough board floors, covered thick with sawdust to absorb the tobacco juice and on occasion the blood of the brawlers, a mixed array of rough men and equally coarse women caroused and careened. Going down Third Street on any afternoon, evening, night or early morning one could hear the shrill music of the fiddle or bag-pipe, the melodeon and accordion, while spiked feet danced in such unison as their maudlin drunk owners could command..."**

Once broke, often within a few days, there was little for shanty boys to do except work in the mills for the long summer until it was time to head for the north woods again in the fall.

No gambler was brave enough to try to take Joe Fournier's roll. Everyone knew Joe because his fierce tricks had left his mark in the saloons. His most famous stunt was to bite a chunk out of a wooden bar with his massive double row of teeth, growling "Dat Joe Fournier, hees mark." That impressed even those not taken with his linguistic skills. Oldtimers said he could jump up, stick his calked boots in the wooden ceiling of a bar, hang for a while, then jerk loose and land on his feet. Joe's calks decorated the ceilings of bars all over town.

Joe was a brawler second to none. He fought with his feet, French-style, as well as with his massive hands. And Joe used his huge, thick-skulled head as a battering ram, giving him a weapon which not only baffled but felled most opponents. Fournier engaged in a historic tussle with Silver Jack Driscoll, of Alma, an ex-convict with an axe to grind for everyone. The fight occurred in a Tittabawassee booming grounds watering hole, the Red Keg Saloon in Red Keg, now known as Averill, near Midland. Brawny Driscoll, standing 6'2" and weighing 210 pounds, was a powerful, bullying giant who delighted in pulverizing smaller lumberjacks. He was famed for applying his calked boots to the faces of his opponents, giving them "logger's smallpox". Subduing Fournier was not such an easy task. The pair of powerful woodsmen grappled for hours in the fight which was reported in newspapers, books, and even memorialized in a painting by a Detroit artist, Max Gerger. So many oldtimers bragged they were eyewitnesses to the fight that the bar would have had to have been three times its size to accommodate them all.

With Fournier's hands around his throat, Driscoll found it impossible to use his superior weight and size to advantage, but he finally broke the grasp by digging his heel calks into the Frenchman's foot. Near the end of the fight Fournier made a desperate lunge, hoping to use the fabled head butt to dispatch Driscoll. Silver Jack was fast on his feet and dodged. Fournier crashed out of control, his head splitting the heavy oak of the bar-or so they say.

Who won the fight remains in doubt. Driscoll was said to have stopped Fournier with a clincher to the solar plexus. Others say Driscoll had had enough and called

SAGINAW RIVER
STEAMBOAT LINE

Steamer **DANIEL BALL.**
  "   **L. G. MASON.**
  "   **CORA LOCK.**

Six Trips Daily between Bay City and East
Saginaw, stopping at all intermediate points.

Offices in Bay City and East Saginaw.

Steamer Daniel Ball, one of a trio of excursion boats plying the Saginaw River trade, is featured in this advertisement in a directory published during lumbering days. Thousands of ships and boats passed through the Third Street Bridge each year in that boom time for Bay City.

it off. Whatever the outcome, at the end Driscoll is said to have treated Fournier as a pal and as though the fight never occurred. Driscoll even bought Joe a double brandy, which leads us to conclude that the fight either was a draw or that Driscoll for the first time gained respect for an opponent. Fournier went to his grave without ever contracting loggers' "smallpox."

Even Fournier didn't survive the rowdiest place of all-aboard the excursion steamboat <u>Daniel Ball</u> from Saginaw. Wesley Hawkins, a Bay City wholesale liquor dealer, put together Sunday trips to Bay View, a picnic spot on Saginaw Bay at Wenona Beach near the mouth of the Kawkawlin River. The trip drew a crowd from several river stops, including Saginaw, Carrollton, Bay City, and Essexville. There was plenty of Hawkins's booze, both on the boat and at a bar at Bay View. One frequent passenger was Rose Barlow, a teetotaling beauty who had been trained as a boxer and was in tip-top shape from working out with dumbbells. Rose was aboard to indulge in her favorite pastime, dancing. If a drunk accosted Rose, she generally knocked him out or overboard. It was said she feared no man and had the strength and fighting skill to back up her courage. There is no account of Joe ever tangling with Rose. He ran afoul of some male cruisers who were not only feisty but also vengeful, as we shall see.

Annette LaFramboise Smith Collection

Hawkins & Company's Dock, where Fournier met his awful fate, is left of the moored excursion steamer. Left are piers protecting the Third Street Bridge. Maxwell's wharf, at the foot of Third, was the point of daily departure for ferries for East Saginaw, Alpena, Sebewaing, Pine River, Banks and Essexville.

Chapter 5
TREACHERY, MURDER END VIOLENT CRUISE, FULFILLING OMINOUS PREDICTION BY JOE

On November 7, 1875, Fabian "Joe" Fournier was knocked into the pages of history to emerge as Paul Bunyan. The sensation caused by the slaying, subsequent trial, and remarkable jury verdict focused public attention on him and his exploits for years. The amazing chain of events leading to memorialization began with an ordinary lumberjacks' brawl and ended in tragedy. Fournier's destiny was to be fulfilled as Paul Bunyan, the greatest French Canadian - and American - hero in all folklore.

The Saginaw Daily Courier got downright indignant about the murder and all that led up to it. The newspaper's local department fed its readers a diet of this kind of news the next day.

A CRUSHING BLOW
Dealt with a Ship Carpenter's Mallet
Caves in the Skull of a Notorious Bay City Rough
And Fells Him to the Earth a Lifeless Corpse
Blinky Robinson Supposed to Have Done the Business
He is No Where to be Found
Arrest of Three Men and Two Women

Bay County Historical Society

Water Street, looking north from Fourth, looks harmless enough, but this was the center of "Hell's Half Mile." Infamous Wolverton Hotel at Third and Water is in background behind hardware and other storefronts, left. Entrance to Hawkin's dock, where Fournier was killed, is between the buildings.

The <u>Courier</u>'s front-page news story on the murder began with an editorialized howl as follows:

> **"Bay City has long been infested with one of the most notorious gangs of ruffians that ever cursed civilization and the damnable outrages they have committed during the past five years would fill a volume. At all times and under all circumstances they have indulged in their nefarious villanies, and if the authorities of that place are not to a certain extent responsible, it is quite certain that had one-quarter of the deeds the gang are guilty of been committed in any other town in the state, the perpetrators would long since have found steady homes in the state prison, or been compelled to emigrate. The terrible murder committed there on Sunday night is the natural outgrowth of such a condition of affairs, and while it shocks the community, it is fortunate that the victim was one of the gang, and met a fate to be expected. How a man could be knocked down and killed in a crowd on a steamboat dock and escape, is a conundrum we should like to have the officers down there explain."**

The steamer <u>Daniel Ball</u>'s excursion to Bay View, a picnic spot on Saginaw Bay, on that fateful Sunday was described by the <u>Courier</u>. "And, as usual, when she reached Bay City a gang of roughs got aboard," the newspaper sniffed. Among the "roughs" were Fournier, French Johnny Gorham, Joe Nichols, and Blinky Robinson (whose real name was later found to be Robertson). The paper continued the grim tale: "While at Bay View they engaged in a wrestle and a fight was the result, Fournier being pitted against Nichols and Gorham against Robertson. After the fight the matter apparently was dropped, and on the boat nothing occurred to recall it except the demonstrations of Fournier, who was so greatly enraged that he went here and there, biting pieces out of the ship's rail, grating his teeth, etc."

Arriving at the dock in Bay City just after dark, Fournier went ashore, and as he staggered down the gangplank someone asked him where he was going. He replied, "To hell," and had proceeded but a few steps when his murderer came up behind and delivered the fatal blow, fulfilling the prophesy of doom. Witnesses at a coroner's inquest the next day said the slayer came up from the side with the mallet in both hands and hit Fournier one blow, saying: "Take that you French --- -- - -- ---!" Johnny Gorham ran after the murderer and was hit in the face with the mallet. The slayer wore a felt hat with tassels, dark clothes and a short coat, reported Gorham, who was covered with blood. Charles Wendell said the killer had a white silk handkerchief with a blue border around his ears and mouth. The man who struck the blow had on a hat similar to the one worn by the man with whom Fournier had fought at Bay View, Wendell said. "I stuck out my foot and tripped him up; he fell on one hand but jumped right up and ran on again," he recalled. Saloon keeper Fred Champaign, who was near the fallen Fournier, said: "I went to pick him up and he was limp as a rag; he didn't appear to breathe, and I thought he was dead."

Joe Fournier was dead—collapsed in a heap on the dock. Dr. J. R. Thomas was called but could do no more than to examine the lifeless corpse. He told the coroner's jury in formal terms that Fournier came to his death by fracture of the skull above the left ear.

"There is no abrasion of the surface, and the fracture must have been occasioned

Bay County Historical Society

Bay City's first hostelry and early hotbed of political activity was the Globe Hotel, in the heart of Hell's Half Mile, Water at Fourth streets, Bay City. This was where the hell-raising crew from the excursion boat was arrested after the murder of Joe Fournier.

by a blow from some blunt instrument; the mallet shown would produce such a fracture." The Saginaw paper reported with editorial comment:

"Fournier was about 30 years old and leaves a wife and two children—a boy aged eight months and a girl two years—at Bangor, where the body of the deceased was taken. He was a powerful man, and had the reputation of being a great fighter. He was a noisy, quarrelsome fellow, drank considerably and in all respects was a notorious rough."

Suspicion rested heavily on Robertson, a stone mason, who was not to be found. He had been seen running in the neighborhood of Eleventh Street soon after the murder and he had a handkerchief around his face, as Wendell testified the man who struck the blow had. Robertson lived at Richard Camber's Stanstead Boarding House on Saginaw Street, between Tenth and Eleventh streets.

Police arrested Joe Nichols, Thomas O'Brien, Maggie "Bricktop" Watson, and Maggie Barnes at the Globe Hotel, at Water and Fourth. All had been implicated in the troubles leading to the murder and were in the Saint James Restaurant after the murder. None tried to escape. A red-goateed suspect, James Wildman of Wenona, was arrested by Officer Nevins of Wenona, who had gotten a telegram across the river from Horace Becker, Bay City Third Ward constable. However, witnesses said Wildman was on the boat at the time of the murder.

A reward of $300 was offered for Robertson's capture. "We understand a horse from his stopping place was missed yesterday and it is supposed he must have stolen it and rode away. He will doubtless endeavor to reach Canada," the Courier opined.

The Bay City Tribune chimed in, indicating the community's growing dissatisfaction with "law enforcement":

> **"The Sheriff has offered $300 reward for the apprehension of Blinky Robertson, the supposed murderer of Fournier. Of course, if the reward is paid the Sheriff expects the county to pay it. Would it not have been better for the sheriff to have attended to his duty as pointed out by the Tribune last summer, suppressed the riotous features of the Bay View excursions, prevented the murder, and thus saved the necessity of offering any reward."**

The coroner's jury sifted the evidence, starting with the fracas at the Bay View. After the wrestle, Joe Nichols boasted that he could whip Fournier, who outweighed him by thirty pounds and was five inches taller. Blinky and another man chimed in and said if he couldn't do it, they'd help him. Johnny Gorham told the jury he and Fournier had tipped a glass or two but weren't drunk. "We knew what we were about."

Nichols's boasts were empty, of course, and Fournier knocked him senseless. Robertson was seen with one eye closed, the other bleeding and with teeth marks on his nose where Fournier applied his massive molars to good effect. Nichols held a handkerchief over his eyes most of the time afterward, Samuel Campbell related. "Joe Nichols was badly used up by the fight at Bay View and was not seen on the boat on the way back," recalled Jim Stevenson.

As the Daniel Ball steamed slowly across moonlit Saginaw Bay and up the broad river toward the lights of Bay City, Fournier had a feeling death was in store for him.

Bay County Historical Society

Excursion steamer, flags flying and a large crowd aboard, is surrounded by sailboats as it traverses Saginaw Bay, appearing much as the Daniel Ball must have during its weekly trips to Bay View in 1875. The rowdy outings to the picnic spot on the bay aroused the ire of the local townsfolk and the daily newspaper, which editorialized indignantly, especially after the murder of Fournier following one trip.

He said as much to Gorham. "No one will kill you, Fournier, while I'm around," French Johnny replied. But when the fateful moment came, Johnny couldn't help. Fournier had been in perfect health. He wasn't hurt in the fight or in coming aboard the boat. Gorham told the jury:

> "I was with him all the time and didn't hear any threats made on the boat. Fournier followed me off the boat; when I got off the boat I saw Blinky Robertson come through the crowd with a maul in his hand; he made a pass at me with the mallet and I dodged it and then he hit me on the head with it; I know it was Robertson; Joe Fournier was struck after I was, I think; I was covered with blood and saw no more of the affair."

Other evidence against Robertson came from Champaign, who ran the saloon under the nearby Third Street Bridge. Champaign told of standing and talking with Fournier on the Hawkins and Company dock for about five minutes after the boat landed and the gangplank was laid. Champaign said:

> "I saw a man coming through the crowd on a run. He was a short, thick-set man; saw his arm or hand come up toward Fournier's head; heard a blow, and Fournier turned toward the man who struck him and fell; the blow didn't sound like one from a man's fist; the man who struck the blow was dressed in black, I think, and wore a short coat; he looked like Blinky Robertson; when he struck the blow he turned and ran; I wouldn't know him if I saw him again."

Advertisement including businesses from many points in Saginaw Country was featured in city directory of Bay City for 1874-75. Lower right is the small ad promoting the Morin House, in Banks, where Fournier and his family lived.

The uncertainty on the part of Champaign and Charles Wendell, a watchmaker, also a witness, later proved a key in the trial.

After taking the testimony of one or two immaterial witnesses, the coroner's inquest jury retired and after an absence of ten or fifteen minutes returned with a verdict in effect that Fournier was killed by Adolphus "Blinky" Robertson.

Saginaw Officer James Nevins and Chief of Police T. Dailey Mower arrested Robertson about 9:15 Monday night in Saginaw. "He was found in a room on the second floor of the Hovey Block, in the southeast corner of the building," the Saginaw Courier duly reported on November 10. "It was known by the officers that Robertson had friends in this city and the vigilant officers were on the watch." A handkerchief covered with blood was found in the room.

Robertson had been in bed and had little to say, although he casually remarked that Bay View was a bad place. He also said that he got up about an hour before the officers came, with the intention of going down home, but went back to bed. "He was taken to Bay City last night by Officers Mower and Nevins, who have thus added more laurels to the honors already won by themselves and the police force of this city," the Courier boasted on Nov. 10, adding:

> **"Robertson has a peculiar expression of the eyes, one eye-lid being partially paralyzed. The left eye was red and swollen, evidently from the blow he received on Sunday. His face also had a red and puffy appearance. He is about 5 feet 6 inches in height, weighs about 150 pounds, and is thick set and well built. His hair is dark and he was dressed in dark clothes. His parents reside below the depot in this city."**

Michigan Photographers Society, Michigan Historical Collections,

Bentley Historical Library, The University of Michigan

Saginaw, where stone mason Adolphus "Blinky" Robertson was found by police and arrested for the murder of Joe Fournier. Saginaw was "jumping off" spot for timber fellers, many of whom hired out from Johnny McDermott's lumber camp employment agency there.

On November 13, the Courier reported that the examination of Blinky Robertson to be held before Justice Nathaniel Whittemore on Saturday afternoon was postponed until the following Tuesday, November 16, on motion of the defendant's attorneys. The newspaper noted growing public interest in the case and displayed some sympathy for the suspect. The crowd moved in as Deputy Sheriff Fred Whittemore brought Blinky from the jail to the justice's office.

> **"Detective Nevins walking in the rear, and to avoid the crowd, which numbered several hundred, so great was the interest felt in the case taking backstreets to reach the justice's office. Blinky looks much better than when brought from jail two days ago, his eyes looking much improved, and his general appearance shows good nursing. His countenance betokens a keener appreciation of his situation, but he is quite reticent and is disposed to little conversation. Incidentally, we learn that preliminary steps have been taken by Fournier's widow, and counsel engaged to prosecute a suit for damages against the proprietors of the boat and all who in any way contributed to the death of Fournier."**

At the examination, the case against Robertson began to fall apart. The headlines of the Daily Courier on November 25 read:

I. H. Catlin Testifies Positively that the Accused
Was On the Boat When Fournier Was Killed
Officer Meyers Thinks One Person Could Not Have Struck All the Blows

Bay County Historical Society

The old Bay County Jail, across Center Avenue from the Court House, boasted a fancy fountain and landscaping with decorative trees. An indication of progressive thinking in Bay City at that time was the fact the jail had separate quarters for women on the top floor and amenities not found in the typical lumberjack lock-up. It was built at the extravagant cost of $35,000, only $5,000 less than the Court House.

Despite doubt cast by respected witnesses (Israel Catlin being a county superintendent of the poor), Justice Whittemore denied a defense motion for a new trial and held Robertson for circuit court trial before Judge Sanford M. Green in the Bay County Court House.

With the Christmas season being at hand, prosecuting attorney G. M. Wilson asked that the trial be delayed; proceedings did not get underway until the new term of court began in late January. The delay proved a key element in the verdict, as it gave Robertson's friends time to generate support for him. Perhaps even the witnesses were influenced, although no charge of impropriety was made.

The jury impaneled January 24, 1876, included Eugene Willett, Donald McDonald, Robert Pontive, Philo B. Root, John S. Reilly, Merritt M. Smart, Edward N. Beebe, Calvin Harrison, Merrill F. Wilcox, John Allan, James Cool, and Arthur Randall. It appears from the names that most were of Anglo-Saxon extraction, as was the defendant Robertson, and none was French Canadian.

Much of the testimony in the trial was merely an elaboration of that given in the coroner's inquest, but there was one new report. Nichols testified that Fournier sang a strange little ditty while in the bar at Bay View. The song went like this, he told the jury:

"Joe was a little man;
Joe was very small;
Joe was a --- -- - -----;
And the bully of them all - me, Joe Fournier."

Did the recollection of Joe's strange song, identifying himself as a bully and a

Annette LaFramboise Smith Collection

Robertson was tried for the murder of Fournier in this imposing old Bay County Court House, with a tower room overlooking the booming lumber town of Bay City and grounds decorated with a Civil War cannon.

--- --- -----, help to turn the opinion of the jury against him and in favor of Robertson? No one will ever know for sure, but it can be assumed this evidence proved damaging to the prosecution.

Champaign and Wendell both continued to waffle, saying they couldn't positively identify the slayer of Fournier. The man who struck Gorham and murdered Fournier looked a little taller than Robertson, Wendell said.

Further evidence was heard January 25th and 26th and the conclusion and closing arguments were made January 27.

The seeds of doubt had been sown in the minds of the jury and there was division of sentiment. On Friday, January 28, 1876, the Courier reported:

THE VERDICT GIVEN
And "Blinky" Robertson Throws
Off the Shackles and Walks Forth
To-Day, a Free Man

"The trial of Adolphus, alias "Blinky" Robertson, who was found secreted in the Hovey block, in this city, on the night of November 9th, and arrested on a charge of having murdered Joe Fournier on Hawkin's steamboat dock in Bay City on the evening of the 7th of the same month, the full particulars of which appeared in the Courier at the time of the occurrence, has occupied the attention of the circuit court at Bay City the entire week. The case went to the jury at 4:30 p.m., yesterday, and at 7 o'clock the jury returned a verdict of "not guilty." We

Annette LaFramboise Smith Collection

From the courtroom, Robertson had this view from the Court House, looking east across rooftops of the imposing homes of lumber barons in Bay City, one of the three fastest-growing towns in America, the others being Denver and Minneapolis.

understand that on the first ballot the jury stood eight for acquittal and four for conviction."

Judge Green therefore ruled:

"The jury heretofore impaneled and sworn in this cause sat together and after hearing the conclusion of the arguments of counsel and the charge of the court retired from the bar thereof in charge of Mr. Martin W. Brock, an officer of the court duly sworn for that purpose to consider their verdict to be given and after being absent for a time return into court and say upon their oath that they find the said Adolphus Robertson not guilty in manner and form as the said people have in their information in this cause charged, whereupon the said Adolphus Robertson is discharged from custody."

"THE LAST ACT IN THE TRAGEDY," as the final story on the incident was headlined a few days later, opined that had Robertson been tried immediately after the examination, he would no doubt have been found guilty. The <u>Courier</u> added, however:

"Robertson's friends left no stone unturned in their efforts in his behalf, and at the trial evidence was produced which raised a doubt in the minds of the jurors and they very justly gave the prisoner the benefit of the doubt. The sentiment of the better class of the community both at Bay City and the Saginaws has been against Robertson, while the sympathy of the mob has been extended to him. While it is better that ten guilty men should escape than that one innocent man should be punished, there are hundreds of persons in the Saginaw valley who will go down to their graves carrying with them the settled conviction that "Blinky" Robertson struck the blow that killed Joe Fournier."

Certainly it would be little solace to Fournier to know that his murderer, Robertson, was consigned to obscurity while he was to become the archetype for one of the most popular legends of all time, Paul Bunyan.

Chapter 6
Tales of Fearsome Fournier's Feats Enliven Campfires; Bunyan Hits Print

So Joe was gone. But the stories about him went on. The publicity of the murder and trial further heightened the imaginations of all who heard the news. Around countless campfires, loggers talked of Joe's amazing feats. As storytellers will, each added something, and most was made up. Some of those yarns were heard later by a young boy growing up in Northern Michigan, James H. MacGillivray. A native of Meaford, Ontario, whose family moved to Oscoda, young MacGillivray went into the woods to scale lumber and be a cook's helper at age thirteen. He heard his first Bunyan stories in Roderick "Rory" Frazer's logging camp twenty two miles east of Grayling on the north branch of the AuSable River. That was the area in which Fournier had been a logger about twenty five years before. Tales of Fournier had merged into stories about one Paul Bunyan, a more familiar French Canadian name.

MacGillivray became a newspaper writer, working for papers in California, Washington, and Alaska in between lumbering and mining jobs. He penned the first Paul Bunyan story in 1906 for the <u>Press</u> of Oscoda-AuSable, Michigan. The story was based on the exploits of timber fellers he had heard about from Jimmy

Conn and other storytellers. The French Canadian aspect had more appeal, so Fournier won out over Driscoll as the primary model for the hero.

The following is the first story in print to mention Paul Bunyan, published in the <u>Press</u> on August 10, 1906, (Vol. 13, no. 34):

ROUND RIVER

****

Reason a log rolls? 'Cause she's round
Pervidin' of course that she's Perfec'ly sound.
If you want a good dog-get a hound!

We'd placed our camps on the river's bank we didn't know it was Round River then and we put in over a hundred million feet, the whole blamed cut comin' off one forty.

You see that forty was built like one of them "Gypsum pyramids," and the timber grew clear to the peak on all four sides. It was lucky, too, that we had such an incline, for after we'd been snowed in, shutting off supplies, Double jawed Phalen got walking in his sleep one night and chewed the only grindstone in the camp. So the boys used to take big stones from the river bed and start them rolling from the top of the hill. They'd follow them down on the dead jump, holdin' their axes on them, which was sharp when they get to the bottom. We'd a shoot for the timber on all four sides and when we was buildin' the last one on the west, away from the river, we comes across a deer runway. "Fourty four" Jones, kindo straw boss, was buildin' the slide, and he liked game. But he didn't say nothin', though I knowed he had an idea.

Sure enough, Jones gets up early next mornin', and he caught the deer comin' down to drink, and he starts the logs down that shoot and kills more'n two hundred of them. We had venison steaks all winter, which went fine with the pea soup.

That pea soup didn't trouble the cook much. You see, we'd brought in a whole wagon load of peas, and the wagon broke down on the last corduroy and dumped the whole mess over into the springs. The teamster came in sorry-ful like expectin' a tote road ticket, but Canada Bill he says to Bunyan, 'Its all right, Paul, them is hot springs.' So he puts some pepper and salt, and a hunk of pork in the springs, and we'd pea soup to last us the whole job, but it kept the flunkies busy a totin' it in from the springs.

That Round River ox team was the biggest ever heard of, I guess. They weighed forty-eight hundred. The barn boss made them a buckskin harness from the hides of the deer we killed: and the bull cook used them haulin' dead timber to camp for wood supply.

But that buckskin harness queered them oxes when it got wet. You know how buckskin will stretch? It was rainin' one mornin' when the bull cook went for wood, and he put the tongs on a big wind-fall and started for camp. The oxes pull all right but that blamed harness got stretchin' and when the bull cook gets his log into camp it wasn't there at all.

He looks back and there was the tugs of that harness stretched out in long (lines) disappearin' round the bend of the road as far as he could see. He's mad and disgusted like, and he jerks the harness off and throws the tugs over a stump. It clears up pretty soon and the sun comes out dryin' up that harness, and when the bull cook comes out from dinner, there's his wind-fall hauled right into camp.

It's a fright how deep the snow gets that winter in one storm, and she'd melt just as quick. Bunyan sent me out cruisin' one day and if I hadn't had snow shoes I wouldn't be here now to tell you. Comin' back, I hit the log road though I wouldn't knowed it was there but for the swath line through the tree tops. I saw a whip-lash cracker lyin' there on the snow. Hello, says I, someone's lost their whip-lash and I see it was Tom Hurley's by the braid of it. I hadn't any mor'n picked it up 'fore it was jerked out of my hand, and Tom yells up, 'Leave that whip of mine alone dam' ye! I've got a five hundred log peaker on the forty foot bunks and eight horses down here, and I need the lash to get her to the landin'.

They was big trees what Bunyan lumbered that winter and one of them pretty near made trouble. They used to keep a compitisun board hung in the commisary showin' what each gang sawed for the week and that's how it happened. Dutch Jake and me had picked out the biggest tree we could find on the west side of the forty, and we'd put in three days on the

Library of Congress

Fifty-four White Pine logs, each 16-feet long, tower skyward as proud timber fellers pose with the huge sleigh load. Incredible loads could be pulled by teams on icy roads which had been sprinkled with water, although two or three teams might be needed to "break" a load free. Real lumberjacks, using only hand tools, were capable of legendary feats such as decking this monstrous pile of timber, called a brag load.

felling cut with our big saw, what was three cross cuts brazed together, makin' thirty feet of teeth. We was gettin' along fine on the fourth day when lunchtime comes and we thought we'd best get on the sunny side to eat. So we grabs our basket and starts round that tree. We hadn't gone far when we hears a noise-and blamed if there wasn't Bill Carter and Sailor Jack sawin' at the same tree.

It looked like a fight at first, but we compromised meetin' each other at the heart on the seventh day. They'd hacked her to fall to the North, and we'd hacked her to fall to the South, and there that blamed tree stood for a month or more, sawed clean through, but not knowin' which way to drop 'til a wind storm came one night and blowed her over.

Right in front of the bunk-house was a monster "schoolmam" what's two trees growed as one, so big she'd'a put the linen mills out of business. Joe Benoit and Dolph Burgoyne used to say their A,B,C's in front of her, and they soon learned to read and swear in English.

You should have seen the big men what Bunyan put on the landin' that spring when they commenced breakin' the rollways. All six footers and two hundred pounds weight. Nothin' else could classify, and the fellows what didn't come up to the regulations was tailed off to burn smudges, just to keep the mosquitos from botherin' the good men. Besides, the landin' men got a double allowance of booze.

From the Collections of the Michigan State Archives, Department of State

Logs spill over banks and clog river as the drive to the booms awaits the peak flow of the stream, when it "ran black and high," as the Round River poem goes. River hogs, using peavies and pike poles for balance, jauntily pose for photographer on the opposite bank.

I'll tell you how it come. Sour faced Murphy was standin' in the kitchen one day lookin worse than usual, and first thing the flunky knowed the water and potato parrin's in his dish began to sizzle, and he saw right away that it was Murphy's face what was fermentin' them. He strained the thing off, and sure enough he had some pretty fair booze which was much like Irish Whiskey. After that Bunyan took Murphy off the road and gave him a job as a distillery.

She broke up early that spring, the river was runnin' black and high, and all hands went on the drive. Bunyan was sure that we would hit the 'Sable or Muskegon, and he cared a dam' for which logs was the same price everywheres.

We'd run that drive for four weeks, makin' about a mile a day with the rear, when we struck a camp what had been lumberin' big and had gone with their drive (what must have been almost as large as Bunyan's). They'd been cuttin' a hill forty, too, which was peculiar, for we didn't know there could be two such places. We drove along for another month and hits another camp and another hill forty, deserted like the last one, and Bunyan begins to swear for he sees the price of logs (sinkin') with all this lumberin'.

Well, (we started) and pulled (them) logs for (five) weeks more and blamed if we don't hit another hill forty, then Bunyan gets wild! "Boys" he says, "if we strike anymore of these dam camps, logs won't be worth thirty cents a thousand, and I won't

Bentley Historical Library,

Michigan Historical Collections, The University of Michigan

Riverhogs pause in the water during a lull in the spring log drive. Riding the logs using peavies to prevent a jam took agility as well as bravery, and blasting the jam with dynamite added another peril. Riverhogs also had to guard against rustlers lurking along the streams to hook stray logs, a practice called "hogging".

be able to pay you off. Perhaps some of you wants to bunch her?
"Lets' camp and talk it over, he says. So we hit for the deserted shacks, and turnin' the bunkhouse corner we who was leadin' butts right into our "schoolmam"!

Then we knowed it was Round River.

The tale starts out with "Fourty Four" Jones as the "kindo straw boss," but thereafter puts Paul Bunyan at the head of the crew. The first character mentioned in the tale, Double jawed Phalen, is a definite link to Fournier who reputedly had a double row of teeth. In the first mention, it is just "Bunyan," which may indicate MacGillivray first heard of the character as Bon Jean. He adds the first name, Paul, apparently as an afterthought in the next sentence.

The origin of the other characters is obscure, but they probably were lumberjacks MacGillivray had heard about while he was working in the woods. The Canadian connection is strong, with Canada Bill, Dolph Burgoyne, Joe Benoit, Phalen, and, of course, Bunyan. Others, such as Jones, Sailor Jack, Bill Carter, and Sour Faced Murphy, represent the traditional Anglo-Saxon populations that dominated the region, and another European, Dutch Jake, appears.

No written mention of Paul Bunyan predates this story by MacGillivray, indicating the tales no doubt originated from oral history. Dozens of reports confirm that Paul Bunyan tales were part of oral history in various logging regions, including Quebec, Maine, Minnesota, Washington, and California. Saginaw pine country, in the AuSable River area, is where the legend first came into print and began to grow.

Chapter 7
Lumberjack Storyteller Jimmy Conn
Spreads the Legends of Paul Bunyan

The most important figure in spreading and perpetuating the oral history of the legend of Paul Bunyan was the lumberjack storyteller, Jimmy Conn. Little is known in the history of lumbering or folklore about Conn's part in popularizing Paul Bunyan. The first writer of Bunyan tales, James H. MacGillivray, who heard the legends from Conn, detailed the connection in an unpublished letter to the chief of the folklore division of the Library of Congress in 1951:

> **"Conn, a little, wizened, log-jobbing Irishman, saw the opening for camp entertainment by rearranging, augmenting or subduing the fabulous feats of one, Paul Bunyan, that were circulating through the Michigan lumberwoods. He had the same subtle style as his prototype, Munchausen, though he probably never heard of that famous falsifier. He soon grew renowned through the Great Lakes timber country as a super tale teller."**

The tall tales of Baron Hyronymus Carl Frederich Munchausen, of Bodenwerder, Germany, were formulated during his twenty years as an officer in the Russian cavalry. Retiring to his substantial country estates near Hanover, the expansive Baron Munchausen regaled friends with war and hunting stories served up with hyperbole and fine pilsner beer.

One of the Baron's guests was a gifted young scholar, Eric Raspe, a Cassel College graduate and curator of the Landgrave of Hesse museum. Raspe compiled the first edition of the Baron's tales as <u>Baron Munchausen's Narrative of his Marvelous Travels and Campaigns in Russia</u>. MacGillivray noted: "The popularity of Haspe's publication was indicated by the printing of more than 100 subsequent editions and numerous attempts by other writers to exploit the Baron's style."

Other literary works may have been influenced by Munchausen, MacGillivray asserted: "In all probability Washington Irving had read the Baron's tales before he wrote about Rip Van Winkle's long sleep. Mark Twain's <u>Jumping Frog of Calaveras County</u> and his <u>Yankee in King Arthur's Court</u> savor of Munchausen." Robert Browning's <u>Pied Piper of Hamelin</u>; the poem by Oliver Wendell Holmes, <u>Deacon's One-horse Shay</u>, and the works of the poet of the Yukon, Robert W. Service, O. Henry, and others reveal similar influences."

As to the place of origin of the Bunyan tales, MacGillivray asserted: "Some of the embryonics of Conn's lumberjack tales doubtless originated in Maine and some in Wisconsin and Minnesota. However, many of the localities that have cited Bunyan as a local character had not even marketed lumber when the AuSable River of Michigan was the banner timber producing stream of America.

"There is little doubt but that most of the tales of Bunyan's prowess as a logger were born in Michigan, or that most of the fabulous stories were either originated

Photo Courtesy Cathy Olsen

Rube Babbitt, Michigan's first conservation officer, regales a group of businessmen gathered at an AuSable River Lodge. Was Babbitt perhaps holding forth about Paul Bunyan? Members of the Smith family of Bay City industrialists who owned the lodge led sportsmen and conservationists in clearing the AuSable of logs and planting 22 million trees on "cut-over" land under Babbitt's influence.

by Jim Conn or regimented by him," MacGillivray averred, continuing: "Tales came in to the AuSable river region, from the Saginaw, the Cass, the Tittabawassee, Menominee, Muskegon, Thunder-Bay, Manistee and other streams. Some were uncouth. Conn would 'make 'em over' with his clever technique, modifying them with nuances of verity."

Conn would indulge in French Canadian impersonation, in the manner of the time, and also was something of a vocalist. "The Jam on Garry's Rock," a tragic tale of a river drive foreman, "Young Monroe," carried away in a boiling flood, was his favorite tune.

Conn was born near Sandusky, Ohio, about 1870 and worked as a small, or "chin-whiskered" jobber on the AuSable for about forty years. He died in the Duluth area about 1940, having apparently carried the Bunyan tales there sufficiently to convince generations of Minnesotans that Paul Bunyan was a native of that state.

MacGillivray reported that academic researchers, particularly W. W. Charters of Stevens College in Missouri, traced the origin of Bunyan to Canada, noting: "French-Canadians on the AuSable would tell you that the name originated on the Miramichi in New Brunswick. Others would emphatically aver that it was born on the Chaudiere in Quebec. Still others asserted that they first heard the name on the Richelieu in the same province."

The legend that originated in Canada picked up new and more amazing details as it spread westerly through the lumbering regions. Bon Jean or the French Canadian word "bongyenne" (of uncertain meaning) became Bunyan while the first name may have come from a Paul Bonhomme of the Two Mountain country, described by Walter Havighurst, who wrote about legends of the Upper Mississippi. ("Bonhomme" means a simple, good-natured man, while Jacques Bonhomme in French usage means a typical rustic person).

Annette LaFramboise Smith Collection

The fast-flowing AuSable River was the stream where logs from Michigan's richly-timbered midsection were floated to Lake Huron at the lively twin villages of AuSable and Oscoda. The legends of Paul Bunyan, centered on this storied stream and featured in newspapers and magazines, launched the tales from campfires to international folklore recognition. Pine "sweepers" which plagued canoeists overhang the stream.

Scandinavian and American Indian elements were added to the original French and Irish aspects of the tales which sprung from old folk stories such as Gargantua and Pantagruel by the French satirist Rabelais. Gargantua, of course, was a character as huge as Bunyan later became, and was first of the "giants" of literature.

Thousands of returning Civil War veterans received land grants in Michigan, and many tried to farm the sandy soil in northern areas without success, some drifting into lumbering or other occupations. Some literary observers think a classically educated Civil War veteran might have combined Gargantua with Bon Jean, the ideal logger, and folk hero Finn MacCool to help create Bunyan in the Munchausen tradition.

Jimmy Conn was a super tale teller in the Michigan lumbering regions, the same areas where Fournier had worked. There is little doubt Conn would have incorporated Fournier's exploits into his Bunyan yarns, later put in print by MacGillivray. For it was on the AuSable, perhaps working for the H.M. Loud Co., that Fournier had served most of his time in the woods. Numerous indications that this is true crop up in the early writings about Bunyan, as will be shown in later chapters. The evidence is circumstantial, but substantially so, that Fournier's exploits and fame were incorporated into the Bunyan tales. Most notably, the character of Bunyan did not take on any particular identity until after Fournier's death; thereafter, Bunyan was a fighter, a drinker and a top timber boss -- just like Fournier. Later, Bunyan's character changed according to the whims of the author of the tale.

Chapter 8
The Bunyan Legend Takes Shape
in a Second Newspaper Story and a Poem

MacGillivray wrote the first Bunyan tale during a short break in his newspaper career while he visited home in Oscoda. A wandering journalist in the Mark Twain tradition, he had worked for the Sacramento Star, the Spokane Review, the Marquette Mining Journal and the Alaska News, joining the Detroit News Tribune staff in 1907, when he was 34 years old. Three years later, on a dull Saturday with little news breaking, News Tribune city editor Malcolm Bingay told every member of the staff to write his own "good story" for the

MacGillivray as a young newspaper writer.

95

Sunday magazine. MacGillivray merely reworked his "Round River" piece from 1906 by adding nine paragraphs at the start and two at the end. It appeared on July 24, 1910, under the new title "The Round River Drive." At the beginning it read as follows:

What! You never heard of the Round River drive? Don't suppose you ever read about Paul Bunyan neither? And you call yourselves lumberjacks?

Why, back in Michigan that's the one thing they ast you, and if you hadn't at least "swamped" for Paul you didn't get no job—not in no real lumber camp, anyway. You Idaho yaps may know how to ranch all right, or pole a few logs down the "Maries," but it's Maine or Michigan where they learn to do real drivin' - ceptin' Canada, of course.

You see back in those days the government didn't care nothin' about the timber and all you had to do was to hunt up a good tract on some runnin' stream - cut her and float her down.

You was bound to strike either Lake Huron or Michigan, and it made no difference which, 'cause logs were the same price whichever, and they was always mills at the mouth of the stream to saw 'em into boards.

But the Round River drive - that was the winter of the black snow. Paul, he gets the bunch together, and a fine layout he had.

They was me, and Dutch Jake, and Fred Klinard, and Pat

MacGillivray's second Paul Bunyan story as it appeared in the Detroit News Tribune Illustrated Section on July 24, 1910. A newspaper artist's conception of a lumberjack telling a Paul Bunyan tale to his compatriots set a colorful scene for the reader.

O'Brien-"P-O-B" and Saginaw Joe, and the McDonalds-Angus, Roy, Archie, Black Jack, Big Jack, Red Jack, Rory Frazer, Pete Berube - oh, we were there some! They was three hundred men all told.

Canada Bill, he was the cook, and two flunkeys were his cookees. We'd a stove, eighteen by twenty, and Paul ust to keep those flunkeys busy in the morning, skatin' round the stove with hams tied to their feet, greasin' the lid for the hotcakes.

And it went fine for a while till one morning "Squint Eyed" Martin, the chore boy, mistook the gunpowder can for bakin' powder, when the cook told him to put the risen in the batter.

Those flunkeys had just done a double figger eight when Paul commences to flap on the batter. Good thing the explosion went upward so it saved the stove. But we never did find the flunkeys - at least not then - cause that was the winter of the black snow, as I told you.

The main portion of the story remained the same as the Oscoda Press version. But the tale ended with a new twist, however:

So we hits for the deserted shacks, and turnin' the pyramid corner, we who was leadin' butts right into - our schoolma'am! And there at her feet was those two flunkeys what had been blown up months ago, and at their feet was the hams! Then we knowed it was the Round River, and we'd druv it three times.

Did we ever locate it again? Well, some!

Romanticized portrayal of river hog on the drive illustrated Stewart Edward White's 1908 novel, "The Riverman." Note crew at work, right. Major parts of the novel were based on events which occurred in Bay City involving river hogs after the drive.

Tom Mellin and I runs a line west, out of Graylin' some years afterward when logs gets high, thinkin' to take them out with a dray-haul, and we finds the old camp on section thirty-seven. But the stream had gone dry, and a fire had run through that country makin' an awful slashin' and those Round River logs was charcoal.

Well, that was the second Paul Bunyan story, all right. It took four years before the third one got into print. MacGillivray got together with a poet, Douglas Malloch, and produced another version of the same yarn, this one in verse. The pair met at a Lakes State Forest Fire Convention at Lansing, Michigan, the state capital, in 1912. Malloch, columnist for the <u>American Lumberman</u> magazine, was known as the "Lumberman Poet." MacGillivray, recalling their joint work, described it as doggerel (irregular or comic poetry). "It was agreed it would run in the <u>American Lumberman</u> as his," MacGillivray wrote to a folklore expert in 1942. The poem, the same as the previous story, was called "The Round River Drive." It appeared in 1914 and provided the first national exposure for the legend of Paul Bunyan.

THE ROUND RIVER DRIVE

'Twas '64 or '65
We drove the great Round River Drive;
'Twas '65 or '64-
Yes, it was durin' of the war,
Or it was after or before.

Those were the days in Michigan,

The good old days, when any man

Could cut and skid and log and haul,

And there was pine enough for all.

Then all the logger had to do

Was find some timber that was new

Beside a stream - he knew it ran

To Huron or to Michigan,

That at the mouth a mill there was

To take the timber for the saws.

(In those days the pioneer

He need not read his title clear

To mansions there or timber here)

Paul Bunyan, (you have heard of Paul?

He was the king pin of 'em all,

The greatest logger in the land;

He had a punch in either hand

And licked more men and drive more miles

And got more drunk in more new styles

Than any other peavey prince

Before, or then, or ever since.)

Paul Bunyan bossed that famous crew:

A bunch of shoutin' bruisers, too-

Black Dan MacDonald, Tom McCann,
Dutch Jake, Red Murphy, Dirty Dan,
And other Dans from black to red,
With Curley Charley, yellow-head,
And Patsy Ward, from off the Clam-
The kind of gang to break a jam,
To clean a bar or rassle rum,
Or give a twenty to a bum.

Paul Bunyan and his fightin' crew,
In '64 or '5 or '2,
They started out to find the pines
Without much thought of section lines.
So west by north they made their way
One hundred miles until one day
They found good timber, level land,
And roarin' water close at hand.
They built a bunk and cookhouse there;
They didn't know exactly where
It was and, more, they didn't care.

Before the Spring, I give my word,
Some mighty funny things occurred.
Now, near the camp there was a spring
That used to steam like everything.

One day a chap that brought supplies
Had on a load of mammoth size,
A load of peas, the bloomin' mess,
Fell in the spring—a ton I guess.
He come to camp expectin' he
Would get from Bunyan the G.B.
But Joe the Cook, and French Canuck,
Said, "Paul, I teenk it is ze luck-
Them springs is hot; so, Paul, pardon,
And we will have ze grand bouillon!"

To prove the teamster not at fault,
He took some pepper, pork and salt,
A right proportion each of these,
And threw them in among the peas-
And got enough, and good soup, too,
To last the whole of winter through.
The rest of us were kind of glad
He spilt the peas, when soup we had-
Except the flunkeys; they were mad
Because each day they had to tramp
Three miles and tote the soup to camp.

Joe had a stove, some furnace, too,
The size for such a hungry crew.

From the Collections of the Michigan State Archives, Department of State

Flunkies trim pies and set the table for the evening meal, preparing for the hungry charge of timber fellers out of the woods at the end of the long work day. Note oil lamp hanging over the table to provide illumination during the after-dark meal.

Say what you will, it is the most,

The pie and sinkers, choppers eat

That git results. It is the beans

And spuds that are the best machines

For fallin' Norway, skiddin' pine,

And keepin' hemlock drives in line.

This stove of Joe's it was a rig

For cookin' grub that was so big

It took a solid cord of wood

To git a fire to goin' good.

The flunkeys cleaned three forties bare

Each week to keep a fire in there.

That stove's dimensions south to north,

From east to westward, and so forth,

I don't remember just exact,

And do not like to state a fact

Unless I know that fact is true,

For I would hate deceivin' you.

But I remember once that Joe

Put in a massive batch of dough;

And then he thought (at least he tried)

To take it out the other side.

But when he went to walk around

The stove (it was so far) he found

That long before the bend he turned

The bread not only baked but burned.

We had two flunkeys, Sam
And Tom, Joe used to strap a ham
Upon each foot of them
When we had pancakes each A.M.
They'd skate around the stove lids for
An hour or so, or maybe more,
And grease 'em for him. But one day
Old Pink-eyed Martin (anyway
He couldn't see so very good),
Old Pink-eye he misunderstood
Which was the bakin'-powder can
And in the dough eight fingers ran
Of powder, blastin'-powder black-
Those flunkeys never did come back.
They touched a cake, a flash, and poof!
Went Sam and Tommie through the roof.
We hunted for a month or so
But never found 'em—that you know,
It was the year of the black snow.
We put one hundred million feet
On skids that winter. Hard to beat,
You say it was? It was some crew.
We took it off one forty, too.
A hundred million feet we skid-

Michigan Historical Collections,

Bentley Historical Library, University of Michigan

Horses (obscured, foreground) pull rope to trip key log in banked timber. Scene is breaking of rollways at Bamfield's at the Alcona Dam Pond on the AuSable River. This was an operation of H.M. Loud Co., of Oscoda, whose logmark was "a peavey with a circle L," Bunyan's mark from the poem. Loud may have employed Fabian Joe Fournier during his brief, stormy lumbering career.

That forty was a pyramid;

It runs up skyward to a peak-

To see the top would take a week.

The top of it, it seems to me,

Was far as twenty men could see.

But down below the stuff we slides,

For there was trees on all four sides.

And, by the way, a funny thing

Occurred along in early Spring.

One day we seen some deer tracks there,

As big as any of a bear.

Old Forty Jones (he's straw-boss on

The side where those there deer had gone)

He doesn't say a thing but he

Thinks out a scheme, and him and me

We set a key-log in a pile,

And watched that night for quite a while.

And when the deer come down to drink

We tripped the key-log in a wink.

We killed two hundred in the herd-

For Forty's scheme was sure a bird.

Enough of venison we got

To last all Winter, with one shot.

Paul Bunyan had the biggest steer
That ever was, in camp that year.
nine horses he'd out-pull and skid-
He weighed five thousand pounds, he did.
The barn boss (handy man besides)
Made him a harness from the hides
Of the deer (it took 'em all)
And Pink-eye Martin used to haul
His stove wood in. Remember yet
How buckskin stretches when it's wet?
One day when he was haulin' wood,
(A dead log that was dry and good)
One cloudy day, it started in
To rainin' like the very sin.
Well, Pink-eye pounded on the ox
And beat it over roads and rocks
To camp. He landed there all right
And turned around - no log in sight!
But down the road, around the bend,
Those tugs were stretchin' without end.
Well, Pink-eye he goes in to eat.
The sun comes out with lots of heat.
It dries the buckskin that was damp
And hauls the log right into camp!

Michigan Photographer's Society, Michigan Historical Collections

Bentley Historical Library, The University of Michigan

A crew of river hogs pauses on a flood dam in the midst of the spring log drive. Shanty boys on the drive also were called river dogs, perhaps because they continually worked in wet, cold and hazardous conditions, akin to the saying "it's a dog's life." However, only the most skilled and hardy fellers won the higher-paying jobs on the river.

That was a pretty lucky crew

And yet we had some hard luck, too.

You've heard of Phalen, double-jawed?

He had two sets of teeth that sawed

Through almost anything. One night

He sure did use his molars right.

While walkin' in his sleep he hit

The filer's rack and, after it,

Then with the stone-trough he collides-

Which makes him sore, and mad besides.

Before he wakes, so mad he is,

He works those double teeth of his,

And long before he gits his wits

He chews that grindstone into bits.

But still we didn't miss it so;

For to the top we used to go

And from the forty's highest crown

We'd start the stones a-rollin' down.

We'd lay an ax on every one

And follow it upon the run;

And, when we reached the lowest ledge,

Each ax it had a razor edge.

So passed the Winter day by day,

Not always work, not always play.

We fought a little, worked a lot,

And played whatever chance we got.

Jim Liverpool, for instance, bet

Across the river he could get

By jumpin', and he won it, too.

He got the laugh on half the crew:

For twice in air he stops and humps

And makes the river in three jumps.

We didn't have no booze around,

For every fellow that we found

And sent to town for applejack

Would drink it all up comin' back.

One day the bull cook parin' spuds

He hears a sizzlin' in the suds

And finds the peelin's, strange to say,

Are all fermentin' where they lay.

Now Sour-face Murphy in the door

Was standin'. And the face he wore

Convinced the first assistant cook

That Murphy soured 'em with his look.

And when he had the parin's drained

Classic Press

Classic Press, Incorporated, used this drawing by William Dempster of "double-jawed Phalen," the Bunyan poem character based on Fournier, to illustrate the "Round River" poem by MacGillivray and Malloch in its 1968 edition of a children's book, "Paul Bunyan." The fictionalized lumberjack in long-johns is chewing up a grindstone using his double row of teeth as described in the poem. The book was distributed under the imprint of Children's Press of Chicago.

A quart of Irish booze remained.
The bull cook tells the tale to Paul
And Paul takes Murphy off the haul
And gives him, very willingly,
A job as camp distillery.

At last, a hundred million in,
'Twas time for drivin' to begin.
We broke our rollways in a rush
And started through the rain and slush
To drive the hundred million down
Until we reached some sawmill town.
We didn't know the river's name,
Nor where to someone's mill it came,
But figured that, without a doubt,
To some good town would fetch us out
If we observed the usual plan
And drove the way the current ran.

Well, after we had driven for
At least two weeks, and maybe more,
We come upon a pyramid
That looked just like our forty did.
Some two weeks more and then we passed
A camp that looked just like the last.

Two weeks again another, too,

That looked like our camp, come in view.

Then Bunyan called us all ashore

And held a council-like of war.

He said, with all this lumbering,

Our logs would never fetch a thing.

The next day after, Silver Jim

He has the wits scared out of him;

For while he's breakin' of a jam

He comes upon remains of Sam

The flunkey who made the great ascent

And through the cookhouse ceilin' went

When Pink-eye grabbed the fatal tin

And put the blastin' powder in.

And then we realized at last

That ev'ry camp that we had passed

Was ours. Yes, it was then we found

The river we was on was round.

And, though we'd driven many a mile,

We drove a circle all the while!

And that's the truth, as I'm alive,

About the great Round River drive.

What's that? Did ever anyone

From the Collections of the Michigan State Archives, Department of State

Logmarks stamped on timber were a symbol of ownership and were protected by law, although thieves often "rustled" logs, cut off the ends and put on their own mark. RYE was used by Wells, Stone & Co. of Saginaw on the Tittabawassee River. As early as the 1880s companies learned that x-raying stolen logs revealed the original marks deep in the wood.

Come on that camp of '61,

Or '63, or '65,

The year we drove Round River drive?

Yes, Harry Gustin, Pete and me

Tee Hanson and some two or three

Of good and truthful lumbermen

Came on that famous camp again.

In west of Graylin' 50 miles,

Where all the face of Nature smiles,

We found the place in '84-

But it had changed some since the war.

The fire had run some Summer through

And spoiled the logs and timber, too.

The sun had dried the river clean

But still its bed was plainly seen.

And so we knew it was the place

For of the past we found a trace-

A peavey with a circle L,

Which, as you know, was Bunyan's mark.

The hour was late, 'twas gittin' dark;

We had to move. But there's no doubt

It was the camp I've told about.

We eastward went, a corner found,

Round River

Computer Art by Brett Radlicki

Many indications support the author's theory that the "Round River" of the Paul Bunyan articles and poems was a circular route involving lakes Michigan and Huron and traversing the state up the AuSable River and down the Manistee River, with a short portage near Grayling.

And took another look around.
Round River so we learned that day,
On Section 37 lay.

Hazen L. Miller, in a wonderful little book entitled "The Old AuSable," published in 1963 by William B. Eerdmans, Grand Rapids, Michigan, notes that both the Manistee and AuSable rivers were arteries of travel by the Indians for centuries. They would come up the Manistee from Lake Michigan to Portage Lake, and then pull over a couple of miles to the AuSable, and then descend to Lake Huron. Miller wrote: "It used to be a great fad mixed with much excitement for boats to start in at Grayling - scow boats - filled with provisions for a trip to the mouth of the river, some 200 miles by water. It was a novel experience keenly enjoyed by hundreds in former days before the dams were built to interfere with the down trip."

Obviously, the "round river" was established by long Indian tradition long before writers such as MacGillivray and Malloch put the fictionalized version into print with their "Round River" poem memorializing the geographical phenomenon.

Chapter 9
Tall Tales Stretch The Imagination
and the Bunyan Legend Grows

So there you have it: two sketchy tales in newspapers and longer doggerel in a magazine that shaped the legend.

"It would thus appear that this best known of the Bunyan tales was the joint product of Mr. Malloch and Mr. MacGillivray, written in their spare time while attending a convention which may have had its boresome moments," folklore expert W.W. Charters wrote in 1944. Like Jack's fairytale beanstalk, the Paul Bunyan legend grew and grew, and grew.

The Bunyan story to this point had only the threads of the tall yarns that would be rewoven later by many storytellers - some would say from whole cloth. The early Paul was a bad guy, like his prototype, Fournier, but later he was cleaned up for popular tastes - like a muddy youngster whose parents got him ready for church.

Paul was a logging boss who was strong and a fighter; these traits matched Fournier's qualifications. As the poem bragged Bunyan was "the greatest logger in the land; He had a punch in either hand, and licked more men and drove more miles..." Like Fournier, "a notorious rough", Bunyan swore and "got wild" when he thought the price of logs were dropping in the poem.

Like Fournier, Paul drank and headed a rough crew: "Paul Bunyan and his fightin' crew...The kind of gang to break a jam, To clean a bar or rassle rum." And his gang fit the lumberjack code of taking care of the helpless, as the stanza concluded: "Or give a twenty to a bum."

To this point, according to the stories and the poem, Paul wasn't big. In fact, he was just about Fournier's size. Nowhere in the first two stories or the poem did it mention that Paul was anything but normal size. He was a boss logger, a top woodsman, a drinker of note and headed a tough, fighting gang - but he wasn't big, like the Paul Bunyan of later legend. Paul's landing crew, described in the first story, all were six-footers weighing 200 pounds - big men for those days but certainly not giant class.

However, this crew was involved in some rather extraordinary events. The pattern of storytellers embellishing the Bunyan tales began immediately, giving an indication of even taller and more incredulous tales to come. First came the pea soup cooked in the boiling spring, where it was mistakenly dumped by the teamster. In the first story there was a wagon load of peas producing enough soup to last the whole job. In the poem the peas had already become a ton or more, providing food for the lumber camp all winter.

The tall tale of the hams strapped to the feet of the flunkeys to grease the griddle of the huge stove, "eighteen by twenty," appears to add a new fanciful element to the second story. By the time it reaches the poem, it takes three forties (120 acres) of timber to keep the fire going in the stove. The stove became so huge that Joe, the cook, couldn't walk around it fast enough to keep bread from burning.

The flunkeys, blown up in the stove by Pink-eyed Martin when he mistook gunpowder for baking soda, were lost in the black snow until spring. The black snow became more colorful in later stories - it turned blue.

The loggers got better, too, as the stories progressed. They lumbered a hundred million board feet of timber, all from one forty acre parcel. That was 500,000 logs, using the loggers' rough estimate of 200 board feet per log or five logs per thousand board feet. (A board foot is a piece of lumber twelve inches square and an inch thick.) Not a bad season's work for one crew, although it was a huge one - 300 men in all, or so the story went. With three sixteen footers per tree, (if all the trees were tall) that would be about 167,000 trees. Of course, they were big trees, the biggest on the forty acres taking three crosscut saws brazed together - 30 feet of teeth - and seven days to cut it.

Another of the first Bunyan tall tales was the killing of 200 deer by loosing piled-up logs on them. The deer, apparently normal size in the story, grew in the poem, their tracks equalling a bear's paw in size.

The Round River ox team, "biggest ever heard of," were tiny ancestors of Babe, the huge blue ox of later Bunyan stories. In the first story, the team of oxen weighed 4,800 pounds. The poem described only a single ox, weighing 5,000 pounds (double the size of each of the first oxen) and able to out-pull nine horses. It took the hides of all 200 deer to make a harness for this ox, already beginning to grow to Babe's proportions. However, the ox had no name and no particular color.

Two of the tales were essentially the same in the stories and the poem, the log pulled into camp by drying deer hides and Sour-faced Murphy, whose face boiled potato peelings into Irish whiskey so that Bunyan gave him a job as a distillery.

Double-jawed Phalen (a corruption of Fabian, probably taken from Fabian "Joe" Fournier), chewed up the grindstone, but the men sharpened their axes by holding them to stones rolling down the hill.

From the Collections of the Michigan State Archives, Department of State

John the Bull, Michigan Upper Peninsula ox trainer, with his favorite team. Oxen, the "bulls of the woods," were slower than horses, but more sure footed, so were favored especially on icy roads. Thus Paul Bunyan's attachment to his blue ox, Babe, had a real basis.

In the poem, some of the tales were actually toned down a bit. The river drive of thirteen weeks in the story became a more believable six weeks in the poem. And the tree sawed through from two sides that didn't know which way to drop disappeared from story to the poem. The same fate befell the logs that were burned and turned to charcoal.

Despite these exceptions, the pattern of tall stories growing each time they were told had been set and American imaginations were about to take over.

Chapter 10
Early Author of Paul Bunyan Books
Reveals the Wellspring of the Legend

While the name Paul Bunyan undoubtedly came from Canada, the core elements of the tales, relating the stories to a real timber feller, came together in the person of Fabian "Joe" Fournier of Bay City, Michigan. The most important early author of Bunyan tales, James Stevens, confirmed the connection of the tales with a real lumberjack in a long interview in 1957 with Elwood R. Maunder, published in the journal, <u>Forest History</u>. Stevens said:

> When my wife and I went to the Lake States early in 1930, we spent the summer in Bay City, Michigan, which was the old sawmill capital of the 1880s when Michigan was the leading lumber producing area of all the world. Of course, in 1930 there were old-timers who survived, from even back into the 1870's who had heard the Paul Bunyan stories in the logging camps and remembered them in some detail and how they were told; but the majority of the old 'jacks did not. They just had them all

Forest History Society

James Stevens, author of Paul Bunyan books, at the typewriter. A lumberjack as a young man, Stevens later did public relations for the forest industry in the Northwest, but decried the lack of time to continue writing. His success was marred by battles with the "academic folklorists" who did not believe the Bunyan tales had begun as folk stories.

confused in their minds with the whoppers, the tall tales, the talk of the ring-tailed roarers—like Mike Fink and Davy Crockett— the lore and the lies that were prevalent everywhere on the frontier in the times of their youth.

Stevens was asked the key question by his interviewer: "Are you of the opinion that there was at one time a real person by the name of Paul Bunyan?" Stevens replied:

I'm sure there was, that there was a name something like "Paul Bunyan" - "Bon Jean" perhaps. I'm sure of it because those things aren't just spun out of thin air. They take root; the seed falls somewhere on fertile soil and the conditions are right and it grows. The right person gets it, builds it up out of reality. H. L. Mencken, the old editor of the <u>American Mercury</u>, and I had correspondence on that proposition. It was his conviction that there was no such thing as folklore per se, but there would be stories that people would tell back and forth and exaggerate on them somewhat, then here would come a born storyteller. He would belong to the people but own a rare gift as a creator of stories. This natural story creator would take bits of simple lore and start creating with them just as the cave men artists took the hunt and began to create from it - the first primitive art. That was Mencken's conviction and I believe it myself to this day. In its spirit I wrote my Bunyan books."

Stevens later in the interview reveals that "the Iron Man of the Saginaw, Joe Fournier," was one of the main characters on which his book was based. He wrote an article about Fournier published in the American Mercury magazine in 1931. "The style of the story and the details are undoubtedly colored by the influence of Paul Bunyan, legendary hero of the woods, whose acknowledged biographer Stevens has become," the Bay City Daily Times commented, linking the pair.

Lee J. Smits, in his colorful column, "Sidewalks of Detroit," in the Detroit News Tribune, reported how Stevens learned of Fournier, indicating how Joe's fame had already blossomed into hyperbole:

> "Captain (Henry J.) Stark of the Bay City fire department told Mrs. Stevens the story of Joe Fournier, the terror of the town 60 years ago. It is said that he would munch beer goblets and spit the splinters at tenderfeet. On a Sunday night boat excursion there was a fight and when 17 men were pulled off Joe it was found that he had expired. Blinky Robertson was arrested because he had a hammer in his hand at the conclusion of the melee. The trial centered about Exhibit A, which was Joe's skull. Blinky went free because it was shown conclusively that the damage to the skull could not have been done by an ordinary hammer. They are still looking for a man who carried a neck poke or a peavey on a Sunday picnic."

Stevens later summed up his experiences researching in Bay City:

"The fact is that there is an endless number of old Bunyan stories, and the ancients have begun to recall them. They had been mainly forgotten after lumbering passed on. Those that were remembered survived only as whoppers. And all the collections of the professors have amounted to no more than a mass of meaningless exaggerations. In them Paul had no character whatever. It was my conviction that in the height of his deacon seat glory he did have as definite a character as the Lincoln of the Lincoln legends. So when I went after the old-timers it was not for stories but for character and form. The woods are full of Bunyan stories. My trouble has not been in collecting them but in escaping them. So I might get nothing from a dozen interviews with old 'jacks. Then I'd hit one who had the sense of character and form which I was sure the best of the old shanty bards possessed. When I had what I felt was the actual Bunyan character, then I was ready to tackle my pile of material. The Saginaw Paul is the true one, I believe. The Western loggers lost the character who was a hero of the pine woods rivers and winter snows. So the Paul of the first book was mainly my own creation. I honestly believe the hero of the SAGINAW PAUL BUNYAN to be at least a true shadow of the Big Feller of the shanties."

Forest History Society

Stevens poses with Bunyan props for another of his books, "Tree Treasure," produced during a prolific career as an author of books and magazine articles about the forest products industry. Distressed by attacks on his first book, <u>Paul Bunyan</u>, published in 1925, Stevens spent a year in Michigan interviewing old lumberjacks about the oral tales and wrote <u>The Saginaw Paul Bunyan,</u> published in 1932.

Stevens later credited William B. Laughead, who also had worked in West Coast camps as a lumberjack in his youth and heard early Paul Bunyan stories, as contributing equally to the growth of the legend. He compared Laughead to intrepid frontiersmen Jim Bridger and Davy Crockett who won just as much fame as storytellers as they did as adventurers. It was Laughead, an artist who did advertising for the Red River Lumber Co. of Minnesota, who gave Paul Bunyan the visual image he is known for even today - as a huge, powerful, brawny-armed logger. This mustachioed, behatted giant even sported a French-Canadian sash, linking the character to our own Fabian "Joe" Fournier and his countrymen who became the most famed of all lumberjacks.

Despite his recollection that the basis of Bunyan lore came from oral history, Stevens admitted making up most of the material in his books. He said lumberjacks demanded new material and "called down" any storyteller who was too repetitious; he was merely following the bunkhouse law against twice-told tales. Since the lumberjacks who told the tales made them up, why couldn't an author do the same? Stevens wondered. Bunyan stories were real incidents exaggerated and amplified to make them more interesting; but they had a basis in reality.

An academic authority who thought Bunyan was based on a real man was James Cloyd Bowman of Northern Michigan University in Marquette. Bowman, author of three Bunyan books, wrote in 1941:

Supposedly the original Paul Bunyan was a "big black" Frenchman, a woods foreman of Canadian origin, with pre-possessing physical prowess. Year after year has added to Paul's physical stature and to his miraculous accomplishments

Paul Bunyan Collection, University of Minnesota Libraries

Drawing by W. B. Laughead for the Red River Lumber Company in a brochure announcing its move to the West Coast, was the first time anyone tried to show what the legendary lumberjack looked like. The graphic characterization helped launch Paul Bunyan's fame nationally.

until he has become the greatest of all frontier heroes. Many of the yarns which were once told concerning earlier heroes have been taken over by Paul as a part of his own accumulating myth.

Another author who visited Bay City to gather material for a compendium of lumberjack legends was Stewart Holbrook, who in the 1940s grilled the local townsfolk about famous characters. He, too, heard Fournier tales and reported on them in his extremely popular book Holy Old Mackinaw: A Natural History of the American Lumberjack. Holbrook fostered the idea that Fournier's jawbone with its double row of teeth was used as evidence at the trial of his alleged murderer, Blinky Robertson, in 1875. That bit of local lore may have been apocryphal, because Fournier had been dead only a few months when the trial was concluded. Holbrook's contention that the jawbone was marveled at by students at the University of Michigan Dental School in Ann Arbor for years is a gruesome report that could not be verified. The only evidence of the disposal of Fournier's body this author could find was the death record noting burial in the pauper's cemetery of St. Joseph's Church. The church was then on Washington Avenue between Second and Third streets in Bay City, but the church cemetery was on AuSable State Road on the west side of the river. The death record was mysteriously dated June 1876- eight months after the murder! Parish records at St. Joseph, which has served Catholics of French descent in Bay City since 1851, show nothing on Fournier even though he must have been accorded funeral rites as a member of the parish.

MacGillivray described Bunyan: "But all the French-Canadians agreed that the early Paul Bunyan was a malicious character and not the beneficent person of accomplishments he later became. He was at first a sort of banshee or hoodoo. If the weather was bad for logging it was Paul's fault. If a woodsman had an accident he laid it to Paul. If a camp foreman bungled a job he hung it on Paul."

The addition of an animal to Paul Bunyan's retinue is fitting, because without the oxen and horses the men would not have been able to harvest the vast North Woods. Oxen were more steady on their feet than horses, ate less and could be counted on as a source of food if necessary in tough times. Babe, the blue ox, was an instant success, becoming almost as famous as Paul Bunyan himself.

Conn would never tolerate a blue ox, or blue snow, as fanciful writers later described. His snow was black, just as he had often witnessed during spring thaws large areas covered with what looked like black gunpowder, "which transformed the original white mantle into a shroud of ebony." MacGillivray says the black snow may have been caused by countless numbers of snow fleas, given the scientific definition Achoreutes Nivicola.

Other writers later backed up claims that Bunyan stories had been told in the woods. "Perry Allen and Bill McBride and Tom Jones, three of my best original sources, all swore they heard Bunyan stories in the 1880s," wrote E. C. Beck, in They Knew Paul Bunyan, published by the University of Michigan Press, Ann Arbor, in 1956, adding: "It is supposed that these stories circulated orally for some years before any of them got into print." Beck wrote: "In fact, Paul Bunyan was mentioned in books before 1900." Stevens said his wife, Theresa, an experienced newspaper reporter, researched in libraries and found nothing on Paul Bunyan until 1914, when the poem was published in the American Lumberman. From then on print material about Bunyan began to appear; stories flowed from old timers, recalling rightly or wrongly, that the tales they had heard were of one Paul Bunyan.

Paul Bunyan Collection, University of Minnesota Libraries

Laughead's drawings soon incorporated a huge Babe, the Blue Ox, who became almost as well known as the famed lumberjack, Paul Bunyan, himself. Stevens created the ox as Bebe, with the French spelling soon becoming Americanized.

MacGillivray pointed out that the soldiers of two wars spread not only Kilroy's name but also Bunyan's. "It is certain that they carried the fame of Paul Bunyan around the world," he wrote. Military men endured an environment similar to that of loggers, with little to occupy their spare time but storytelling - and telling tall tales was their favorite entertainment. They, too, needed a powerful symbol who could help them forget their oppressive situation.

This is why Paul Bunyan is America's favorite - a hero claimed by several states as their own. His legend is a folkloric memorial to men who tackled incredibly difficult tasks every day, risking their lives and often losing them, for small rewards and no hope for anything but more unrelenting work.

The stories about Paul Bunyan are outlandishly exaggerated but the man the legend is mainly based on - "Joe" Fournier - was as real as the job the timbermen themselves accomplished - cutting the timber to build a nation.

Chapter 11
Bon Jean To Bunyan:
Americanization of a French-Canadian Hero

One of the earliest books on Bunyan, by James Stevens in 1925, mentions the "mighty-muscled, bellicose, bearded giant named Paul Bunyon" as a character of Canadian origin. Note the spelling. The accent in the last name was on the "yon," pronounced roughly similar to "Jean" by the French. His fame was won in the Papineau Rebellion of 1837, a revolt of French-Canadians against the British crown. In the Two Mountains country, at St. Eustache, rebels armed with mattocks, axes and wooden forks stormed into battle, among them the bearded giant named Paul Bunyon. Stevens wrote:

> **"This forest warrior, with a mattock in one hand, and a great fork in the other, powerful as Hercules, indomitable as Spartacus, bellowing like a furious Titan, raged among the Queen's troops like Samson among the Philistines. He came out of the rebellion with great fame among his own kind. His slaughters got the grandeur of legend."**

Canadian history does not mention Paul Bunyon, but the oral tales about Paul Bunyan could have sprung from "Bon Jean," the hero of the Papineau Rebellion. Farmers and timber cutters armed with nothing but rustic tools, challenging the Queen's well-equipped troops, are the stuff of legend, if not of military victory. The ill-fated rebellion was quickly put down and rebel leaders were captured or fled to the United States. The heroic Bon Jean may have escaped to become an early lumber camp boss in the U.S. where he would make his mark more vividly in history books as Bunyon, a giant of American folklore. After the rebellion this <u>Paul</u> Bunyon operated a logging camp, as Stevens told it. There was no more famous camp chief than Paul Bunyon, who could carry 500 pounds on portage. Stevens also writes of Joe Murfraw, or Murphy, an Irish-French Canadian logger:

"His feats in camp and on the log drives were magnificent. Many old French Canadians have sworn to me that he put the calks in his boots in the shape of his initials and that after the thirteenth drink he would kick his initials in a ceiling eight feet high."

Shades of the famed Joe Fournier, the timber feller best known for performing that trick! The first name and the feat seem to be a direct connection to Fournier as the model for Bunyan. Does he become more Americanized, perhaps, as an Irish French Canadian?

What of Babe, the famed blue ox? Born in Stevens's first book "Bebe," a calf with a French name found in a blue snow blizzard, the change to "Babe" is in the spirit of "TRUE AMERICA," Stevens wrote.

Bowman commented on Paul Bunyan's part in the development of the American

Paul Bunyan Collection, University of Minnesota Libraries

Laughead's ox, Babe, first depicted as almost normal size, grew and grew until it was many times larger than Paul Bunyan. This exaggeration is an example of the way the legend was being blown out of proportion and part of the reason why detractors were able to discredit it.

spirit: "Paul Bunyan yarns are an outgrowth of the soil, and as such are the most fundamentally American of all our folklore."

Not only was Bunyan a direct outgrowth of American frontier life, the tales also were given a definite literary quality by Stevens, who recalled in his interview in Forest History:

> "I had succeeded in taking all this rough stuff of Paul Bunyan and working it over and getting it into a form of literary art. It was literary art that I had achieved, that appealed to Mencken and Knopf. This was the spirit then in which I wrote my first book of Paul Bunyan stories. Mine was the method that I knew Homer had used; that is, the basic stuff of his Iliad and Odyssey was the common folklore of the people of Greece, just as the folklore of the Mississippi River formed the basic material of Huckleberry Finn. I though of it in those terms because my hero and master, H.L. Mencken, considered Huckleberry Finn the greatest American work of literary art.

Expanding on the Americanization of Bunyan, Stevens continued:

> Only in a few regions and among the elders, do the creations of this art, this folklore, survive as shining memorials to sturdier and nobler days. And the legend of Paul Bunyan is certainly the greatest of these creations; for it embodies the souls of the millions of American camp men who have always done the hard and perilous pioneer labor of this country. It is true American legend now, for Paul Bunyan, as he stands today, is absolutely

American from head to foot. He visualizes perfectly the American love of tall talk and tall doings, the true American exuberance and extravagance.

The timing is right to coincide with tales first told in United States lumbering regions about 1850. These stories were a combination of French braggadocio and Irish fancy and sly humor. No doubt they were brought by French Canadian immigrants who had heard of Bon Jean or Paul Bunyon and retold the tales told in the logging camps. Claims that the tales were of Scandinavian, Russian, Native American, or other derivation can be accepted because apparently all eventually were incorporated into the legends of Paul Bunyan. Much as was the case with other immigrants, Paul Bunyan quickly became a true American in the melting pot that assimilated the legends as well as the peoples of the world.

No less an authority than Funk and Wagnalls Standard Dictionary of Folklore, Mythology and Legend, edited by Maria Leach (New York: 1972), sums up the origin of the Paul Bunyan legend:

> **"As far as can be determined the legend originated in Canada during the last century, and was considerably amplified as it spread west and south with the lumber industry, centering in the Lake states and the Northwest. In the course of his migration Paul Bunyan incorporated elements of local heroes like Jigger Jones (Johnson), Joe Mufraw and Jean Frechette, whom he supplanted. To the original French and Irish elements were also added Scandinavian and Indian elements."**

Stevens' <u>Paul Bunyan</u> is a compilation of twelve fanciful tales. In The Winter of the Blue Snow, Paul Bunyon finds the blue ox, named Bebe', and then Americanizes both their names, becoming Bunyan and Babe. Bunyan's curse, "By the holy old mackinaw," re-emerges in Stewart Holbrook's 1943 book, Holy Old Mackinaw: The Natural History of the American Lumberjack.

In "The Bull of the Woods" chapter Bunyan recruits the giant Swede Hels Helsen, "taller than a tree," to help him log virgin Dakota country near the Mountain That Stood on its Head, a peak buried in the ground with trees upside down. Stevens' protagonist "Battling Paul Bunyan" subdues Helsen in a terrible brawl but the duo remain pals, ala Fournier-Driscoll. "You're going to be a good foreman, now, Hels Helsen!" Bunyan proclaims.

The MacGillivray-Malloch poem is recalled when Section 37 is left in the river and washes away. In "The Sourdough Drive," the cook's mixture causes the lake to rise so high logs thunder down the Red River valley.

The Saginaw Paul Bunyan seven years later is an embellished collection of eighteen short stories. Like Fournier, Bunyan hails from Quebec, logs up the Big Auger river, a twisting stream like the AuSable, "and then won his supreme fame in the Saginaw timber country."

Paul rescues shanty boys and tames the wild Big Auger river which had attacked the log banks, hunts wierd creatures such as the swigging mince and the goebird for a thanksgiving meal and uses whales which had jumped Niagara into the Great Lakes to carry logs on the drive. He frees the whales which are related to carp, found everywhere in the Saginaw Valley.

The New York Herald Tribune commented: "Stevens combines the original shanty-camp legends of Paul Bunyan with 'forest-born inventions from the seeds of old lore.' The mighty woodsman emerges as the unequaled hero of American forklore, taming the wilderness and ruling men with incomparable humanity."

Stevens was the author of many books, including Homer in the Sagebrush and Brawnyman.

<u>Chapter 12</u>
Fabian "Joe" Fournier as Paul Bunyan
Becomes Our Favorite Folk Figure

MacGillivray's story was the first in print on Bunyan, writers on the subject agree. However, confusion reigns on when the oral tales of Bunyan sprang up. Most evidence indicates the stories go back to the 1860s, beginning about the time Canadian immigration to Michigan was increasing and Joe Fournier was heading his crew in the woods.

Researchers concur that the tales did not meld into a universally known Paul Bunyan legend until after MacGillivray's articles and the poem appeared, which I believe bolsters the theory that Fournier was the model for Paul Bunyan. Joe Fournier had the right stuff around which a legend could, and did, develop. MacGillivray, building on the tales of storyteller Jimmy Conn, transformed Joe Fournier, along with elements of Silver Jack and others, into Paul Bunyan. Esther Shephard and James Stevens in their books, one published soon after the other, launched Paul Bunyan into public awareness and national popularity. Stevens, after gathering Fournier lore in Bay City in 1930, pinned down the origin of Bunyan in Saginaw Country, indicating a sure link to fabled fighting Fournier. The rest, as they say, is history.

Now to the question of conflicting claims about Bunyan's origins. W. B. Laughead, promoting Minnesota's Red River Lumber Company, helped to spread the legend by adopting Paul Bunyan as the company's mascot. More than 100,000 pamphlets were circulated beginning in 1914 and vastly popularized the giant logger as he "announced" the company's move to the West Coast and "sold" Red River lumber products. Minnesotans adopted Bunyan as their own but Californians saw him as a woodsman in the Northwest.

Laughead's drawing of Paul on the Red River Lumber Company pamphlet with the words "Paul Bunyan's Pine" was the first time anyone tried to show what the legendary lumberjack might have looked like. The company used the drawing as its registered trademark. The advertising booklets published by Laughead in 1914 and 1916 were continued by Laughead's expanded "Paul Bunyan and His Blue Ox" booklets in ten editions from 1922 through 1940.

Laughead drew on his recollections of life in Minnesota logging camps in the early 1900s and bits and pieces of Bunyan lore from letters, columns in West Coast newspapers and the 1914 poem in <u>American Lumberman</u>.

Other lumbering states wanted Paul Bunyan for their own. Wisconsin quickly picked up on the Bunyan stories after publication of the poem in 1914 in <u>American Lumberman</u> provided the first national exposure for him. K. Bernice Stewart and Homer A. Watt wrote about Bunyan for the Wisconsin Academy of Arts and Letters in 1916. They are also credited with doing the first research into Bunyan stories. Stewart and Watt recounted tall tales by lumbermen of the Midwest and Northwest, but the authors admitted the tales were adapted to include Bunyan since not all were about lumbering. This led to more confusion about the origin of Bunyan and obviously gave rise to claims that Paul came from Wisconsin. Soon storytellers from

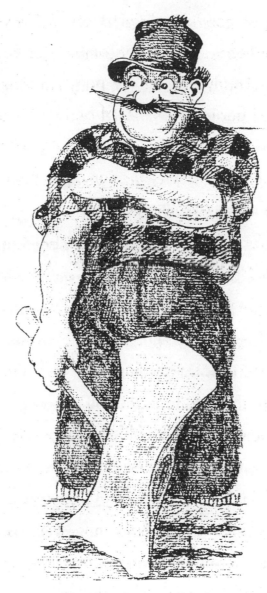

Paul Bunyan Collection, University of Minnesota Libraries

Paul Bunyan rolled up his sleeves and readied his double-bitted axe for a big chopping job in this version of the mustachioed logger by Laughead. Most artists later gave Bunyan a beard, as well.

many lumbering areas avered they had heard Paul Bunyan stories in their part of the country. Shephard's 1924 book, first about Paul Bunyan, was based on stories collected from lumbermen in the Northwest, and added to the confusion about Paul's origin. Shephard commented on the origin of the Bunyan legends:

> **Evidence points to a French Canadian origin among the loggers of Quebec or northern Ontario. But other evidences point just as strongly to an American beginning possibly in Michigan or Wisconsin. Certainly the stories resemble those other frontier stories which were told in that time, back in the 30s and 40s when western humor was at its height and when the most extravagant tales circulated, such, for instance, as those stories which were told of Davy Crockett. It is likely that part of this stream of western humor which filled such a large part of the literature of those early days, crowded out of the main channel by the excitment of the Civil War time, may have found its outlet in the great Northern woods and turned itself naturally into Paul Bunyan legends. Many of the tall tales of the early frontier have been taken over bodily and made into Paul Bunyan yarns.**

Shephard wrote that the oldest of the Bunyan stories dates to the 1860s and perhaps even earlier, reaching their height in the 1880s and 1890s. Stevens reported that Leonard Day, a leading Minnesota lumberman, gained fame as a reciter of Paul Bunyan tales in the 1860s and 1870s. Many of the stories were told to baffle greenhorns, like sending a new employee after a left-handed monkey wrench or a new recruit to get a roll of red tape. Some of the Paul Bunyan stories told in the camps were vulgar or obscene and thankfully never reached print. This greatest of American heroes has been portrayed as largely exemplary, if exaggerated.

About the same time as Shephard's first book was published, James Stevens concocted a story about the "Black Duck Dinner," in which Paul charmed a flock of ducks out of the sky and trapped them in a giant tarpaulin he had spread on the ground. The tarp looked like a lake and Paul gathered the quacking flock to make a Sunday meal for his loggers. The famed writer and editor H. L. Mencken published that incredible tale in his American Mercury magazine and gave Stevens backing for his first book, Paul Bunyan, published in 1925.

Writers followed the tradition of never telling a Bunyan story as it was heard. "Some of their results are a tax on the best imaginations," wrote Gladys J. Haney in the Journal of American Folklore in 1942. She summed up the first twenty five years of Bunyan stories as follows:

> **The Paul of old was a giant in stature, a super lumberjack, and a recognized leader of men in the woods. Today, he is credited with digging Puget Sound, being an oil man in the Southwest, building the Panama Canal and being in service overseas with the A.E.F. At least three writers interpret Paul Bunyan as the spirit of America. Another goes so far as to make him a villain, and a fifth pictures him as of ordinary stature to most, but a giant to those who believe in him.**

Paul Bunyan Collection, University of Minnesota Libraries

Laughead drawing shows Bunyan cutting down a whole stand of trees at the same time, amazingly without the help of another sawyer.

While folklore expert Haney considered the Laughead pamphlets of 1914 as the first written accounts of Bunyan, W. W. Charters told the folklore world in 1944 that Bunyan originated in a Detroit News Tribune article of 1910. We have seen that it was actually in 1906 that Bunyan's name first appeared in print in MacGillivray's first version of "Round River" in the Oscoda (Michigan) Press weekly newspaper.

From 1906 to 1931 Bunyan inspired at least seventeen full-length books (five of them poetry) several plays, vocal and instrumental music, comic strips, ballets, murals, woodcuts, paintings, and statues.

Paul moved around the country in these stories. He changed jobs. A wife and family were acquired. He got a Southern buddy, Tony Beaver. He joined the Army in 1942 and helped the war effort.

By 1929, the Encyclopedia Brittanica included Paul Bunyan and he was chosen as the subject of academic theses. Famed poets Robert Frost and Carl Sandburg wrote of Bunyan. Stevens's 1925 Paul Bunyan became grand opera librettos by two noted composers. A version by Richard L. Stokes, then music critic for the New York Post, was published in book form by G. P. Putnam and Sons. In 1941, W. H. Auden, the British poet, wrote a libretto based on Stevens's book. Benjamin Britten, a British composer, wrote a Paul Bunyan overture and the score for a grand opera produced at Columbia University.

By the late 1950s, Stevens's Paul Bunyan had sold 252,000 copies (140,000 in pocket books through military post exchanges during World War II) but Stevens lamented that the work had earned him only about $18,000.

Literary observers had varying opinions concerning Paul Bunyan and his place in folklore. Wrote Haney: "Some compare him with Hercules and Thor; others prefer to call him a Munchausen." Criticism began in earnest in 1940 when

Paul Bunyan Collection, University of Minnesota Libraries

One of the most fantastic of Laughead's drawings shows Bunyan as an ordinary-size logger astride snowshoes and carrying a double-barreled shotgun while chasing a wolf with its backside turned up. The creature, half wolf and half "elephant hound," was raised on bear milk and called "Sport, the Reversible Dog." Sport was cut in two by Paul by mistake and patched together backside up, which proved an advantage since Sport could run on either side and never tire - he caught everything he ever started after.

Carleton C. Ames wrote an article, "Paul Bunyan-Myth or Hoax" for the journal <u>Minnesota History</u>. Ames points out incongruities in the stories and pronounces Paul Bunyan a hoax.

As Paul Bunyan's popularity grew, criticism increased, mostly from folklore specialists who themselves had compiled books and apparently found distressing the intense and widespread public interest in Paul Bunyan instead of their "correct" folklore. Professor Jan Harold Brunvand of the University of Utah, in his <u>Study of American Folklore</u>, explained:

> "Folklorists tend to exclude as spurious or contaminated any supposed folklore that is transmitted largely by print, broadcasting or other commercial and organized means without an equally strong interpersonal circulation. American folklorists sometimes use the term "fakelore" (coined by Richard M. Dorson in 1950) to disparage the professional writers' contrived inventions and rewritings - like many Paul Bunyan stories - which are foisted on the public as genuine examples of native folk traditions, but which have only a thin basis of real tradition underlying them."

Stevens later commented:

> "I felt that in the way I wrote the Paul Bunyan stories that I would not get involved with the specialists in folklore because by the time I got into the field a little bit I realized that that was a distinct academic field; and so, in writing my Buyan tales as my own stories I wouldn't get into any conflict with professional, academic folklorists at all. But here came these violent objec-

tions from one professor after another - they objected to my touching the Bunyan material in any way whatsoever. So there is a certain attitude of that kind - I won't say that it's a taint - but nearly every professor in whatever field is 'tetched' with it a little bit. "

Some writers on folklore state that Paul Bunyan is one of America's greatest myths. The mythical quality was described by Bowman: "He was so strong that he could hold a buffalo bull out at arm's length. So true was his aim that he could put a bullet through the moon with his faithful old squirrel rifle." Of Bunyan's greatness Bowman commented:

"Many lesser heroes came and went with the years, and it was not until after the Civil War that Paul Bunyan burst like a meteor upon the horizon. The Industrial Revolution was sending thousands of men into the forests, and the forests again released the restraints of civilization, and refired the imagination. The lumberjacks found refreshment for their spirits by capping the biggest yarn their bunkmates could spin. They laughed until the great trees of the forest echoed their refrain."

Around the nation, the legend of Paul Bunyan has caught the interest of Americans through the years. His has been described as the supreme myth of the American people, a creation myth. And it is said that in ancient times he would have been considered a divinity.

In a sense he is divine among our nation's family of legendary characters because Paul Bunyan predates and overshadows Jim Bridger, Pecos Bill, John Henry, Mike Fink, Joe Magarac, and other spirits of the frontier and working world of America. In fact, he may be the psychic father of those other heroes. The Paul Bunyan legend has received a comic interpretation and, at the same time, a most serious one. He is a creator, an inventor, a worker, a builder, a patriot, and a performer of mighty deeds as well as a comic figure we can laugh at and with.

Widely honored as a national symbol, there are dozens of Paul Bunyan festivals, including those in Oscoda, Michigan, and Bemidji, Minnesota. Companies, such as the Paul Bunyan Meat Company, and the Paul Bunyan Motel, both in Michigan, have taken his name. The Red River Lumber Company even changed its name to the Paul Bunyan Lumber Company in Susanville, California. The world's largest wood carving, of sequoia, is of Paul Bunyan and greets visitors to Sequoia National Park in California. Statues of Paul and Babe, his blue ox, abound. Testifying to Paul Bunyan's continuing popularity is the fact that a hue and cry arose when a giant statue of him which had deteriorated over the years recently was dismantled in the Oscoda, Michigan, city park. Townsfolk immediately rescued, repainted and restored the figure. The University of Michigan and Michigan State University football teams still battle each year in a gridiron tussle over the Paul Bunyan trophy.

Although the literature on Bunyan has greatly diminished since 1950, the story remains strong in the American consciousness because of the great store of past literature and popular media as well as a Walt Disney cartoon which has appeared on national television networks for the past decade. Entitled "Three Tall Tales," the cartoon features Professor Ludwig Von Drake hosting an animated special featuring the legends of Paul Bunyan, Windwagon Smith, and Mudville's celebrated Casey

Giant sequoia depiction of Paul Bunyan, carved by Carroll Barnes from a solid piece of sequoia, guards the entrance to Sequoia National Park in California and is said to be the world's largest wood carving.

at the Bat. In the Disney production, Paul Bunyan is described as "the biggest and tallest legendary character of them all," perpetuating the comic interpretation. Here's a summary: Bunyan tales begin around the potbellied stove; the more stories were told, the more he grew. America was a great big land with a great big job to be done. Off the coast of Maine a howling was heard and townsfolk found a great big boy in a huge cradle. It was Paul Bunyan, who grew to sixty three axe handles high with his feet on the ground and his head in the sky. The whole town named him Paul Bunyan. He was so big they raised the roof of the schoolhouse. Other kids jumped off him at the swimming hole. The whole town gave him a double-bladed axe for Christmas and he showed his gratitude by clearing the land for farming. The town had enough timber to last a lifetime. Paul left, saying he would write soon, to become straw boss of a lumber crew in the Midwest. After a career creating rivers and mountain ranges out West, Bunyan passes into another life. The Northern Lights are Paul and Babe knocking the Aurora Borealis out of the sky, according to the Disney production.

As we have seen, the first stories of Paul Bunyan are based on factual exploits-many of which involved Fabian "Joe" Fournier, the terrible timber feller of the Michigan woods. Fournier was the human prototype of Bunyan. Paul Bunyan became through literature more than just a glorified Joe Fournier; he became the personification of the spirit of the American working man. Therefore, Paul Bunyan is not a myth, he is real. However, the writers of Paul Bunyan tales and other commercial promoters like Disney made the character too much larger than life with imaginative interpretations. Paul Bunyan's very popularity became his undoing, bringing jealous charges of fakelore.

Thankfully, America still clings tenaciously to its most enduring legendary hero.

The legend lives and may again thrive. Most Americans from childhood on continue to treasure Paul Bunyan stories. They undoubtedly remain some of the most appealing and popular tales in American literature.

It would be more than just sad and might even prove injurious to the American spirit to lose Paul Bunyan as our hero. We might just as well abandon Santa Claus. It's time to put the fakelore dispute in the past and recognize Paul Bunyan's timeless appeal as an immigrant worker who succeeded in the best American tradition, triumphed over his oppressive environment, and became our sustaining symbol of strength, fortitude, and endurance, growing from a real lumberjack to a legendary hero for children and adults alike.

Long live Paul Bunyan!

NOTES ON THE RESEARCH AND WRITING
OF THIS BOOK

Chapter 1

<u>15-</u>Charges that Paul Bunyan stories are "fakelore" were first brought by noted folklore expert, Richard M. Dorson from the University of Indiana, who wrote an article, "Folklore and Fake Lore," published in the <u>American Mercury</u> in 1950. Jan Harold Brunvand of the University of Utah, another academic authority, concurred with Dorson in a 1959 book, <u>American Folklore</u>, and purged Paul Bunyan from his history of folklore. Even the chief of the folklore division of the Library of Congress, Duncan Emrich, (a.k.a. Blackie MacDonald) attacked the Bunyan legend as fakelore In 1972.

The defense was launched in 1952 by Daniel Hoffman in <u>Paul Bunyan: Last of the Frontier Demigods,</u> noting long oral tradition before the tales first circulated in print. Edith Fowke, in a paper, "In Defense of Paul Bunyan," presented at the American Folklore Society meeting in Portland, Oregon, October 31, 1974, asserted: "Paul Bunyan was not a fakelore invention and he is not a fake folk hero, despite the misuse of his tradition by popularizers." However, the charges of fakelore denigrating Paul Bunyan have caused a loss of his popularity since the Dorson-Brunvand attacks. Some encyclopedias dropped any reference to the discredited Paul Bunyan, although he has since been reinstated.

The term Saginaw Joe, indicates that Fournier was from the Saginaw River area of Michigan. Saginaw County at one time stretched from the present Genesee County all the way north to the Straits of Mackinac, prime lumbering area. Also, Fournier's home was first known as Lower Saginaw (present-day Bay City, including Banks). Interestingly, the polling place for Hampton Township, stretching north for nearly 100 miles, was at the Globe Hotel, Lower Saginaw's first hostelry, which plays a role in the murder recounted in this book. Lively politics centered on the Globe, especially at election times, when ballots were cast by throwing slips of paper into a hat.

16-Many Union Army veterans received grants of seventy five dollars and 160 acres in Michigan as a bonus at their mustering out. In northern areas, some veterans tried to farm the sandy soil but soon gave up, selling the property to railroad companies or logging interests who proceeded to harvest the timber with a "cut and get out" policy.

Two groups engaged in the fur trade, the licensed trader and the coureur-de-bois, the lawless trader. The coureur-de-bois were looked on as "outcasts of all nations and the refuse of mankind", also as "Frenchmen who fraternized with the Indians", and as "soldiers of fortune, gentlemen of no fortune, and plain vagabonds".

Just prior to his death, Fournier lived in the Morin House, listed in an old city directory as located on Main Street in Banks. The building survives and its address is now 1014 Marquette Avenue in the Banks area of Northwest Bay City, according to Barbara Dinauer of the Superior Abstract Co., Bay City, who researched old records of the building. In recent years the two-story frame structure was known as Banks Hardware. The city directory listed Fournier as a ship carpenter employed by J. M. Ballentine & Sons, shipbuilders, located on the nearby banks of the Saginaw River. Ship carpenter was no doubt his summertime occupation when he was not heading a logging crew. According to the directory, Ballentine employed many residents of the village. Why Fournier was not in the woods in November, as normally would have been the case for a lumber camp foreman, is a mystery. However, in 1875 Fournier may have been unable to find work either at the shipyard or in timber cutting, the nation being in the midst of an economic depression which had begun in 1873.

19-The deacon's seat refers to the area where men sat around the fire in the camboose; the dulcey was a primitive banjo-like instrument. Some fellers were persuaded to tie on a hanky and impersonate a woman for dancing purposes.

21-The Third Street dock was the main ferryboat dock in Bay City. The steamer that carried Fournier to his death had picked him up on the Hawkins and Co. dock between Third and Fourth streets. Ironically, Fournier was killed with the very tool he used daily, a ship carpenter's mallet.

Chapter 2

23-Among Army surveyors in Michigan was Robert E. Lee, later to win fame as the Confederate commander in the War Between the States, as well as Jefferson Davis, president of the ill-fated Confederate States of America. The surveyors were offered deeds to land in Michigan, but all turned the offer down flat, pronouncing it the most worthless real estate they had ever seen.

25-Little is generally known in the Saginaw Valley of the fate of the Sauk Indians. It is said the Sauks who survived the massacres and were exiled to Wisconsin were so few in number they merged with the Fox tribe for protection, becoming known as the Sac and Fox. A good account of the massacres is found in a book entitled "Wah Sash Kah Moqua," by Mary Sagatoo, published in Boston in the 1850s, featuring rare tales of her marriage to a Bay County Indian chief and life among the Chippewa at Saganing in Arenac County

Old Morin House, the hotel where Fournier lived, in recent years was the Banks Hardware and now is a warehouse. It was one of more than 100 hotels and boarding houses in Bay City, home to thousands of transient workers during lumbering days. While not in the woods, Fournier worked at the nearby Ballentine shipyard on the river.

for thirty years.

The famed Sauk chief, Black Hawk led his people in the 1832 Black Hawk War in Illinois in a futile attempt to reclaim lost land along the Rock River. Abraham Lincoln fought in that war as a young lieutenant and Jefferson Davis saw combat, too, as the U.S. Army drove the Sauks and Foxes out of valuable farming land coveted by white settlers. That second massacre of the Sauks marked the end of tribal dominance of the woodlands of the west. In an 1867 treaty, the Sauks led by the noted peacemaker Keokuk and the Foxes led by Chekuskuk, ceded 157,000 acres of land along the Mississippi and Missouri Rivers in exchange for $26,574 and 750 square miles of land on a reservation in Indian Territory, later to become Oklahoma.

28-Visiting Oklahoma in 1982, the author inquired of local historians about the Sauks and was referred to the Oklahoma Indian Commission. "If the Sauk Indians survive, they are in Oklahoma," my source at the Southern Production Institute said. "Why?" I asked. "Because most of the tribes sided with the South in the Civil War and were exiled to Oklahoma, which became known as Indian Country," he replied. (Actually, the banishment of Native Americans to Indian Country began long before the Civil War, about 1830.) I found the Sauk (Sac and Fox) reservation halfway between Oklahoma City and Tulsa in a town named Stroud. Interviewing the chief, Jack Thorpe, son of famed athlete Jim Thorpe, I discovered to my amazement that he and his tribe knew all about their history in Saginaw Country. Questioned about how there could be an awareness of events occurring more than 300 years before, Thorpe said,"Oh yes, we have oral history going way back." On the wall in their small tribal museum is a picture of a 1910 baseball team with a player named "Saginaw Grant." Another oldtimer's nickname was the "Sturgeon." No sturgeon exist in Oklahoma, so the name no doubt came from Saginaw Bay, once home of the giant sturgeon fish. The Sauks are thriving as well as any Indian tribe in Oklahoma and have an extensive development, including a museum, rodeo grounds, recreational vehicle park and administrative complex on their reservation of 980-acres. They operate a small campground and earn royalties from twenty oil wells. Their numbers have remained fairly constant at 2,300, compared with their peak of 3,500 in 1650. Thorpe was trying to have his father's Olympic medals returned. They had been confiscated because of the elder Thorpe's alleged violation of Olympic amateur regulations for playing baseball for money. Jack Thorpe was also trying to obtain the return of his father's body from the town of Jim Thorpe, Pennsylvania, formerly known as Mauch Chunk. The medals recently were returned, but the body remains buried in the town square.

29-The settlers of Frankenlust were Germans from Franken, in Bavaria. Nearby are Frankenmuth, Frankenhilf, Frankentrost and other communities settled by people from the same region.

33-deTocqueville's path was followed 150 years later by Richard Reeves, syndicated newspaper columnist. Reeves visited the Bay City area and updated deTocqueville's view in his book, "American Journey."

34-A U.S. Coast Guard official recently commented on Saginaw Bay's status as a dangerous body of water after the bay claimed seven lives in two weekends. Waves on the shallow bay have a great tendency to capsize boats because of the degree of angle created when they hit, the official said. There is no evidence LaSalle ever fulfilled his promise to build a chapel to St. Anthony in gratitude for his deliverance from the raging waters of the bay.

Chapter 3

37-"Daylight in the swamp," or dawn's first light, was the work whistle of the lumber camps. The men were up by four or five o'clock, had breakfast and readied tools. Teamsters began at three o'clock to haul the required number of loads of logs to the banking grounds. Since they started work before daylight and never quit until dark, the shanty boys never saw the camp in daylight except on Sundays.

Although Joe Fournier, alias Paul Bunyan, was a lumber camp boss at the time of his death, it is assumed he began his career as a timber hewer. No doubt he made his mark in a short time and was promoted to head the crew which probably included up to 100 men. Many camps served tea in the English tradition instead of coffee. "Shorts" referred to short logs or loads that didn't measure up. Swampers, who cleared the swamps while building roads from the cutting areas to the river, figure in the second Paul Bunyan story by James H. MacGillivray. The author chides the Idaho men (he calls them "yaps" for not being real lumberjacks if they haven't "at least swamped for Paul") The term "lumberjack" was not used in the early days and seems to have evolved in the 1890s, when lumbering in Michigan was in decline. "Jack" was a generic term for a man, used mainly by saloon girls, barkeeps and other townsfolk.

Fellers, butters, buckers, and skidders refer to the timberman's jobs while cutting in the woods. First the trees were felled by the fellers, then ends were squared by butters, limbs removed by buckers, and the logs slid to the riverbank, usually on icy roads, by skidders using teams of horses or oxen. The travois was a pair of poles hitched to the horses on which logs could be hauled, although wooden sleds with steel runners were most often used in later years.

"Gabriel time" refers to the large horn, used by the cooks to call the men to the evening meal. Syrup was a rare treat when offered for dessert in the camps. Two dozen men often lived in a single shanty. Whistling, singing, and conversation were the sort of entertainment the shanty boys engaged in while in camp after a lonely day in the woods, so a noiseless evening was unusual.

Jack Thorpe, former tribal chief of the Sauk Indians and son of the famed athlete Jim Thorpe, displays some of his father's trophies, medals and memorabilia at the Sac and Fox (Sauk) Reservation near Stroud, Oklahoma. Amazingly, through oral history the Sauks have preserved information about their habitation in Saginaw Country over 300 years ago.

Chapter 4

43-Wearing a bright red sash on holiday to dress up their ordinary work duds was a characteristic of the timbermen of French Canadian origin.

Much has been written about the proclivity of timbermen to cut loose on a spree at the end of a logging season. Dorson, in his book <u>Bloodstoppers and Bearwalkers: Folk Traditions of the Upper Peninsula,</u> published by Harvard University Press, 1952, notes timbermen have been aptly styled "whiskey-fighting men." They followed the lumberjack code calling for them to brawl and get insensibly drunk. He wrote: "Every spring when camp would break, a jack must leave the woods where he has lived in monastic seclusion for six or seven months, hike to the nearest town, and blow his entire stake of four or five hundred dollars on rotgut whiskey. During this spree he visited the brothels and mauled other jacks. When he was dead broke he made his way back to camp, to recoup his stake by working as a river-driver (or river hog). Many jacks never escaped the woods because they blew every stake they made for liquor." Rigid custom dictated that jacks must buy drinks for all at the bar or be known as a "Dick Smith" - a cheapskate. Derivation of the term is unknown, though it may be assumed that it started with a "cheap" lumberjack named Dick Smith.

45-A good description of actual goings on on Bay City's Hell's Half Mile during its heyday is by Stewart Edward White (1873-1946) in his novel, The Riverman, published by Grossett and Dunlap in 1908. He recalled stuffy and squalid saloons, gambling halls run by bold and unscrupulous proprietors with drinks served by "pretty waiter girls." White, who worked in lumber camps and wrote in the early morning before going into the woods, observed: "The pickings were good. Men got rich very quickly at this business. And there existed this great advantage in favour of the dive-keeper: nobody cared what happened to a riverman. You could pound him over the head with a lead pipe, or drug his drink, or choke him to insensibility, or rob him and throw him out into the street, or even drop him tidily through a trap-door into the river flowing conveniently beneath. Nobody bothered— unless, of course, the affair was so bungled as to become public. The police knew enough to stay away when the drive hit town. They would have been annihilated if they had not. The only fly in the divekeeper's ointment was that the riverman would fight back. And fight back he did, until from one end of his street to the other he had left the battered evidences of his skill as a warrior."

White tells of gangs of fighters employed in McNeill's joint on Saginaw Street (probably Scotty Maguire's) using sandbags dropped from a window and brass knuckles on the carousing rivermen. His hero, Orde, however, poses a desperate challenge, foils the professional gamblers, and wins a $500 bet in a brace game (fixed card game). Then he orders drinks for all and escapes the inevitable knock-out drops by spilling out his whiskey and taking another man's drink. "Go easy, and show up at the booms Monday," Orde cautions his crew after the debacle. White calls the town "Redding," but it undoubtedly is Bay City. A similar account with less detail occurs in another White novel, The Blazed Trail, published by Grossett and Dunlap in 1902. There he tells of forty saloons within a radius of 300 feet from Bay City's Catacombs and describes Polly Dickson, the queen of the second floor, "pretty and fresh-faced and at the same time one of the most ruthless and unscrupulous of the gang." The orgy at midnight at the Catacombs "was like hell let out for

Was this business building in downtown Bay City once the notorious "Scotty Maguire's Alhambra" gambling den? At Maguire's, few gamblers were successful but winners were drugged or sandbagged from upper stories as they left the building and stripped of their cash. The athletic Rose Barlow lived in a flat here as Mrs. Hank Smith and was known to sweep her smaller husband's money off the table and drag her chagrined spouse out of the gambling hall by the scruff of his neck.

noon," wrote White, commenting: "The respectable elements of the towns were powerless. They could not control the elections."

47-The long believed, but unconfirmed, rumor in Bay City was that the Catacombs had a slide where drugged or drunken lumberjacks were dropped into the river. An old member of a pioneer Bay City family wrote in a 1981 letter to the author: "Speaking of the St. Laurent building, across the street (Third and Water) stood a somewhat similar structure, a hotel called the Wolverton or Wolverine, I don't remember which, (it was the Wolverton) with as unsavory a reputation as the St. Laurent building, which at that time (1800-1900?) was a resort of entertainment for anyone who had money to spend and catered especially to river hogs with a craving for excitement. The first floor was devoted to selling booze with painted ladies mixing with the customers. The second floor was for dancing and the third floor had beds to accommodate the patrons of the other two floors with their lights of love. The crowd was pretty rough but the security guards (burly pimps) were generally able to handle anything that came up. The girls, too. Anyway, if anyone became too obstreperous or had a roll he was loath to part from it was a simple matter to knock him in the head and slide him down a tunnel into the river. Now this was told to me by my uncle: 'In doing some repair work to this old building, behind a brick-walled partition we came upon a slide that led up to the third floor wide enough to accommodate a sliding body.' Could this building have been the Catacombs of legend?"

"Resorting" was the term for prostitution; laws against it were ignored just as was the prohibition against the sale of liquor, Michigan being dry during much of the lumbering era.

54-The widespread propensity of the timbermen to fight was reported by an old resident of Sanford, in Midland County. At the site of the Tittabawassee Boom Company operations, upwards of 200 riverhogs were seen fighting at one time, the fray having started as each crew tried to get its logs to the boom first. The Red Keg Saloon at nearby Averill was the site of the famed fight between Fournier and Silver Jack Driscoll. Billy McCrary, the original Redkegger, owned the saloon and was himself known as a tough customer with his fists. Red Keg was the setting for two lumber-era novels, the Red Keggers and The Man from Red Keg, by Eugene Thwing.

56-Bay View was later changed to Bayside, apparently to avoid confusion with another Bay View, near Petoskey.

Chapter 5

59-The <u>Saginaw Daily Courier</u>, being published just twelve miles away from Bay City, devoted much of its coverage to happenings in that down river community whose economy, so much like its own, depended on lumbering. Pioneer newspapermen Henry S. Dow, Edwin T. Bennett, and George W. Hotchkiss worked at various times on the <u>Courier</u>, the <u>Bay City Journal</u>, the <u>Bay City Observer</u> and the nation's first lumber trade journal, the <u>Lumberman's Gazette</u>, sometimes holding employment on publications and with a lumbering firm simultaneously.

61-The steamer Daniel Ball was operated by the East Saginaw and Bay City Line in

Evidence of tunnels in the catacombs region is uncovered during recent sidewalk work on Water Street in the famed "Block-o-Blazes" of lumbering times. Tunnels may have allowed saloonkeepers to escape to hotels or horses and avoid being waylaid outside their establishments. Blocked-up doors are in the basements old bars and other buildings on Water and Third streets. Several of the old lumberjack hotels along the waterfront are now antique shops.

---

tandem with the L.G. Mason. The steamers made several round trips daily from Saginaw to Bay City, about 12 miles each way, during the week. The Ball also made special Sunday excursions to Bay View sponsored by the liquor merchant, Hawkins. Some of these trips became rowdy, drunken brawls, and one ended in a murder which proved to have historic significance.

"French Johnny" Gorham was still brawling, although for pay in prizefights, as late as 1882.

Bay View, the scene of the fracas that led up to the murder of Fournier, is now known as Wenona Beach. Newspaper accounts of the fight there mention a bar at Bay View, but no other information has been found about this old bar. An excellent photo book by James R. Watson of Bay City, entitled Wenona Beach reports the beach first had a steamer dock and picnic site and was known as Reservation Beach. It became the Bay View Resort in 1870s, then Oa-at-ka Beach. From 1889 to 1969 the fifty acre beach was the site of the Wenona Beach Amusement Park, including a casino that attracted celebrity talent such as the Marx Brothers, W. C. Fields, Perry Como, Bob Crosby, the Dorsey brothers, Jack Benny, Isham Jones, Ted Weems, and Guy Lombardo. The Bay View Bar, Patterson at Zimmer roads in Bangor Township, is the only place, except on old state maps, that perpetuates the name of Bay View at Wenona Beach.

64-Robertson lived at Richard Camber's Stanstead Boarding House on the west side of Saginaw Street between Tenth and Eleventh streets. The boarding house is long gone and the site now is an automobile dealership.

71-The murder of Fournier drew intense public attention because it was the only slaying recorded in a three year period, historian Kilar reports. Of course, bodies were found in which the cause of death was unknown.

There is no record of any lawsuit filed in Bay County Circuit Court by Mrs. Fournier, whose first name is not known.

74-The old red brick Bay County Court House was built in 1868 and was the county's first such structure. It stood on the northwest corner of Madison and Center avenues. It was torn down in 1932 and replaced in 1934 by the nine-story granite Bay County Building, which stands today on the same site.

75-Jeremy Kilar, of Midland, Michigan, a Delta College historian specializing in lumbering, points out what may be a key element both in the general apathy of townsfolk toward exploitation of timber fellers and in the jury's acquittal of Robertson for the murder of Fournier: many timbermen were immigrants and were scorned by local residents, many of whom were New Englanders, imports themselves. When local workers struck the huge mill of absentee owner Henry Sage in Bay City in 1872, Sage fired them and replaced them with immigrants. During the depression years of 1873-74, immigrant Poles and French Canadians were hired by other mill owners, further alienating the citizenry. Because of the exploitation by mill owners, "Bay City became a community of Polish, French and German enclaves isolated ethnically, geographically and economically," Kilar writes. This lack of a sense of community led to labor unrest which has plagued the city's history. The economy of Bay City was further hamstrung by the failure of moneyed interests to reinvest in job-renewing enterprises after the pine was gone. This was in contrast to Saginaw and Muskegon where paternalistic resident mill owners financed economic diversification, Kilar says in his book, <u>Michigan's Lumbertowns: Lumbermen and Laborers in Saginaw, Bay City and Muskegon, 1870-1905,</u> published by Wayne State University Press (1990).

Chapter 6

79-The "Creator of Paul Bunyan," James H. MacGillivray, Sr., was the son of William and Margaret MacGillivray. He was born May 24, 1873, at Meaford, Ontario, and came to the U.S. with his parents and a brother a few years later. The family located first at Richmondville, Sanilac County and moved to Oscoda in 1881. Brother Will MacGillivray became publisher of the <u>Oscoda Press</u> and served in the state House of Representatives.

After serving as a cook's helper and lumber scaler for Rory Frazer's logging camp, MacGillivray enlisted in the Spanish-American War, but his company was never sent abroad. He became a lumber broker for Great Lakes cargo shipments at age twenty one. Then he prospected in the Northwest and Alaska and managed sawmills in Idaho and Nevada before beginning his newspaper career.

In 1911, after a disastrous fire that destroyed the twin towns of Oscoda and AuSable, ending lumbering in the AuSable River area, MacGillivray was called to state service by Governor Chase Salmon Osborn to head the new Public Domain Commission, forerunner of the Department of Natural Resources (DNR). MacGillivray organized students in Northern Michigan schools into the Michigan Forest Scouts, who served as auxiliary fire wardens and planted more than 200,000 pine seedlings in a reforestation program. As director of the DNR's educational division for seventeen years, MacGillivray traveled and lectured extensively on conservation and fire prevention. He made ten films on wildlife that were shown to nearly 40,000 persons in 1927, his last with the DNR.

MacGillivray then operated James MacGillivray Studios, featuring wildlife films. He also was a wildlife photographer, had a story and photos on beaver published in <u>National Geographic</u> magazine, and did the first study of the rare Kirtland Warbler. He also operated an insurance and real estate business and served as supervisor and treasurer of Oscoda Township.

MacGillivray and Amanda Fiedler of Holt, Michigan, were married June 23, 1913. She was a former superintendent of the Oscoda school system. They had two daughters, Amanda Tripp, of Hollywood, Maryland, and Jean Barton, of Danville, California, and a

Photo courtesy the family of James H. MacGillivray

James H. MacGillivray, author of the first Paul Bunyan tales in print, is cranking away as a wildlife photographer for the Michigan Department of Natural Resources.

son, James MacGillivray. MacGillivray died May 1, 1952 at age 78 in Alpena (Michigan) General Hospital, after suffering a stroke and falling at the Iosco County Court House, Tawas City. He is buried in Oscoda Cemetery.

80-In "Round River," the first character mentioned is "Double jawed Phalen," which no doubt is taken from Fabian "Joe" Fournier, who was reputed to have a double row of teeth. The fact that Fournier is mentioned first in the first story would seem to be evidence that MacGillivray had heard of the famed fighter and used him as a primary model for the Bunyan stories. The stories became confused and overlapped in the continual telling but there is little doubt that Jimmy Conn had included Fournier exploits in his storytelling.

81-The hot springs where the loggers make pea soup is perhaps adapted from the largo Springs, on the AuSable River near Oscoda, between Cooke Dam Pond and Loud Dam Pond. It is not a hot springs, but sometimes appears to be boiling.

86-A clear indication that the Round River actually was a route including the AuSable and Manistee rivers and around Lake Michigan into Lake Huron occurs, in the story: "Bunyan was sure that we would hit the 'Sable or Muskegon, and he cared a dam' for which logs was the same price everywheres." The 'Sable is the town of AuSable, on Lake Huron, while Muskegon is on Lake Michigan. Those two major lumber markets could reached by traveling in either direction, portaging the one mile from the AuSable River into Lake Margarethe and Portage Creek to the Manistee River near Grayling or vice versa. The Indians had another route from lakes Michigan to Huron, following the Grand River to the Maple with portage to Saginaw River tributaries into Saginaw Bay.

Chapter 7

89-The author had never heard the name Jimmy Conn mentioned in connection with lumberjack tales or Paul Bunyan until the unpublished 1951 letter from MacGillivray to Duncan Emrich, folklore chief of the Library of Congress was discovered during research for this book. The letter was in on file in a folder marked "Paul Bunyan" in the American Folklore Room. Emrich himself was not a supporter of the Paul Bunyan tales as true folklore. In his book, Folklore on the American Land, Boston: Little Brown and Co. 1972, Emrich wrote: "The dividing line between legend and tale is occasionally a slim one. Then why not allow Paul Bunyan to join the group? Simply because Paul Bunyan stories (with very few exceptions) never have circulated as folklore. They have been the creation of newspapermen, writers, public relations men for the lumber companies, local chambers of commerce, and others. They have circulated in print, and rarely orally. A very cursory reading (three or four pages) of James Stevens's (no relation to the poet) 'Paul Bunyan' will clear the air in this respect. The person looking for folklore in the tales will back away from them in sharp anguish. (There is, to return to an earlier observation, no folk language or speech in them. It is impossible to believe that these stories were ever told.)"

90 - MacGillivray wrote that the Au Sable was the "banner timber producing stream of America." However, Saginaw historian Stuart Gross notes the Tittabawassee and Muskegon rivers were first and second, respectively, in logging activity.

Chapter 8

96-The second Round River story mentions in the fourth paragraph how logs could be floated either to Lake Huron or Michigan, reinforcing the theory that the Round River was the route through the AuSable and Manistee rivers.

The black snow makes its debut in the fifth paragraph, and Saginaw Joe, another reference to Fournier, is mentioned in the sixth paragraph along with Rory Frazer, a definite connection to the early oral tales because Frazer was the owner of the lumber camp where MacGillivray had worked as a boy.

102-The poem, being the joint work of MacGillivray and Douglas Malloch, mentions some new lumberjacks, including "Patsy Ward, from off the Clam," probably referring to the Clam River in Oregon. Joe is the cook in this version, Double-jawed Phalen returns, and Jim Liverpool appears and "makes the river in three jumps." Silver Jim (the poets probably meant Silver Jack), Harry Gustin, Tee Hanson, and others also appear. (Hanson is the name of a family of Grayling, Michigan, pioneers.)

111-A grindstone, as chewed up by "double-jawed Phalen," is a unique Michigan product linked to a town in the Thumb region, Grindstone City.

117-"West of Grayling 50 miles," mentioned in the poem would be the Traverse City area.

Paul's logmark, the peavey with the circle L, is the mark of the Loud logging interests of Oscoda, the company Fournier may have worked for at one time.

Malloch also wrote a poetic version of the song, "Michigan My Michigan." Born in 1877 in Muskegon, Malloch was known as "The Lumberman Poet."

Chapter 9

121-It is interesting to note at this juncture that the first two Paul Bunyan stories and the poem are seldom mentioned in criticism of the tales as fakelore. This chapter notes that the tales began on a somewhat conservative note but that writers immediately began to embellish the tales. The fanciful books on Paul Bunyan seem, in the minds of critics at least, to have completely overshadowed the first three print articles, which certainly qualify as folklore. The situation is somewhat understandable, as the newspaper articles were published in a provincial weekly and a state daily, and the American Lumberman had circulation primarily in the lumber trade, although it was national in scope.

Most of the lumberjacks were rough and uneducated, but others, in the tradition personified by the French Foreign Legion, founded in 1831, were fugitives, failed professionals or cultured social outcasts judged in the lumber camps only by their ability

PAUL BUNYAN'S

FABULOUS EXPLOITS

BORN ON AuSABLE RIVER
IN 1860'S

PERPETUATED IN FIRST
WRITTEN NARRATIVE

"ROUND RIVER DRIVE"
BY JAMES MacGILLIVRAY
DETROIT NEWS TRIBUNE
1910

TRANSPOSED TO DOGGEREL
BY DOUGLAS MALLOCH
AMERICAN LUMBERMAN
1914

"---,FOR, IN THE AIR, HE
STOPS, AND HUMPS, AND MAKES
THE RIVER IN THREE JUMPS!"

SPONSORS: ELTON R. EATON
COMMUNITY PROGRESS CLUB

Plaque donated by civic group in Oscoda commemorates oral history of Paul Bunyan and MacGillivray's perpetuation of the character in print but fails to mention the first article in the local Oscoda, Michigan, weekly newspaper in 1906. The bronze plaque on a stone base is located in the city park on U. S. 23 highway in Oscoda.

with a saw, peavey, axe or driving a horse team.

Chapter 10

127-The Bay City connection is one of the most important in tracing the tales to Fabian "Joe" Fournier. Stevens did his research there and later wrote "The Saginaw Paul Bunyan," which was his report to the literary world that his research had revealed that Paul Bunyan was from the Saginaw region.

A confusing element arises in the Maunder interview in Forest History, in which Stevens claims to have invented Joe Fournier. In writing his books, he said, "I used all of Laughead's principal characters. I thought up a number of rivers, then John Shears, the boss farmer, Shanty Boy, and the Iron Man of the Saginaw, Joe Fournier, Little Meery, Mark Beaucop-invented in France, 1918-Jonah Wiles, who was the enemy of Sourdough Sam. Offhand, I just can't remember any more." This bolsters my belief that writers were much like the tellers of oral tales-many stories were mixed up, attributed to the wrong characters, etc., because of the telling and retelling by many people. He admits in the interview that he can't remember who told the tales to him but that all the Paul Bunyan tales came from the Great Lakes states and nowhere else.

Stevens also believed there were seven or eight Silver Jacks. "It seemed that after the first Silver Jack - I'm sure that he's never been tracked down by any researcher - anyone who was a big, tough fighter in a sawmill or logging town would be called Silver Jack."

Stevens reveals in the interview that his wife, Theresa, a former newspaper writer, researched the files of the Lumberman's Gazette in the Bay City Public Library (now in the Michigan Historical Collections, Ann Arbor), the American Lumberman and the Northwest Lumberman, back to the 1860s but could find nothing in print on Paul Bunyan. After 1914 many articles were written on Paul Bunyan because by then the copying and building on MacGillivray's and Malloch's work had begun in earnest.

133-Bowman's reference to a "big black" Frenchman indicates a swarthy, almost black complexion peculiar to some people of Gallic origin.

Chapter 11

139-Stevens related in his interview about the origin of the Paul Bunyan tales that he had consulted academic authorities at a Roman Catholic college in Quebec who were unable to find any reference to Paul Bunyan in connection with the Papineau Rebellion. Other writers contacted the Montreal Public Library, where researchers came to the same

ERECTED TO PERPETUATE THE MEMORY OF THE
PIONEER LUMBERMEN OF MICHIGAN THROUGH
WHOSE LABORS WAS MADE POSSIBLE THE
DEVELOPMENT OF THE PRAIRIE STATES

Lumberman's Monument in the Huron National Forest, near Tawas City/East Tawas, in Iosco County, has been viewed by countless tourists. Erected in 1932, the three bronze figures honor a river driver, left, a timber cruiser and a tree feller, right. Robert Ingersoll Aitkin's nine-foot sculpture is located on the high banks of the AuSable River thirteen miles northwest of East Tawas and the same distance west of Oscoda.

dead end. Stevens said he and his wife "searched lumber publications and pine-town newspapers, in the hope of finding documentary evidence on Paul Bunyan to please the Ph.D.'s. We found nothing better than an occasional item on the 'sogger,' the 'sidehill-gouger,' the 'hodag,' and other animals remindful of the imaginary memories of Jim Bridger and the cowboys who came after him."

143-In addition to Jimmy Conn, another storyteller, Jack Rabiot of Tawas, crops up in Stevens' correspondence with Lee J. Smits, a Michigan newspaper columnist and public relations man. In the introduction to his book, "The Saginaw Paul Bunyan," Stevens writes: "My authorities remain Z. Berneche, Louis Letourneau, Michael Christopher Quinn, Rube Babbitt, Jack Rabiot, Tod Fox and a hundred old "pinetops" of Michigan, Maine, Oregon and other lands of timber and clearings."

A broader view than Emrich's regarding Paul Bunyan is expressed by Maria Quinlan of the State Museum of Michigan, writing in 1978: "Another legacy evident today is the body of songs and stories about lumbering, an important part of the folklore tradition of Michigan, and indeed, of the entire nation."

Chapter 12

146-Laughead, advertising his Minnesota (later California) lumber company, used oral tales from lumberjacks as the basis for his material, too, according to Stevens. His part in the popularization of the legend through advertising was perhaps more important than that of the books which followed. More than 100,000 copies of Laughead's booklet, <u>Paul Bunyan and His Big Blue Ox</u>, were published in twelve editions. After an initial mailing to the pine trade in 1922, no copies were sent out except upon request, according to a 1943 article in the American Lumberman. Archie D. Walker, then president of the Red River Lumber Co., was credited with the initial idea to use Paul Bunyan in the firm's advertising. Both Laughead and Walker reportedly had heard Paul Bunyan tales in the lumber camps. The article states that Paul's name was familiar to only a limited number of pine loggers prior to 1914. The Red River Lumber Co. was later named the Paul Bunyan Lumber Co. and is located in Susanville, CA.

148-Esther Shephard actually wrote the first book about Paul Bunyan, in 1924, but Stevens, whose book was second, in 1925, seems to have attracted more attention. However, Shephard seems to have gotten more critical acclaim for her account of the Bunyan legend, apparently considered real literature, while Stevens was accused of exaggeration from the first and his book denounced by academics. Stevens's correspondence with H. L. Mencken, while writing the book showed definite concern about Shephard beating him into print. Extensive correspondence between Stevens and Mencken and Mencken and publisher Knopf is located in the Paul Bunyan Collection of the University of Minnesota Libraries and was consulted in the writing this book.

Shephard's name is sometimes spelled Shepherd, and for good reason; she married two men whose names were pronounced the same but spelled slightly differently. Through most of her literary and academic career she was known as Esther Shephard.

Shephard mentions a P.S. Lovejoy of Ann Arbor, Michigan, in the preface of her book. Stevens also mentions a Professor Lovejoy of Michigan State College in his interview with Maunder in <u>Forest History</u>, noting that his work in interviewing old lumberjacks about the Bunyan legends ought to be preserved and studied, although Lovejoy's work came after the MacGillivray articles.

149-Gladys Haney noted that one observer who commented favorably on Shephard's book saw the tales as a mixture of ancient mythology, daydreaming, real American humor and an attempt to impress the credulous greenhorn.

Bibliography

Books

Brunvand, Jan Harold. The Study of American Folklore. New York: W. W. Norton Co., 1968.

Dorson, Richard M. Bloodstoppers and Bearwalkers: Folk Traditions of the Upper Peninsula. Cambridge: Harvard University Press, 1952.
American Folklore. Chicago: University of Chicago Press, 1959.

Hoffman, Daniel. Paul Bunyan: Last of the Frontier Demigods. Philadelphia: University of Pennsylvania Press, 1952.

Holbrook, Stewart H. Holy Old Mackinaw: A Natural History of the American Lumberjack. New York: Macmillan Company, 1943.

Miller, Hazen L. The Old AuSable. Grand Rapids, Mich.: William B. Eerdmans Publishing Co., 1964.

Reimann, Lewis C. When Pine Was King. AuTrain, Mich.: Avery Color Studios, 1981.

White, Stewart Edward. The Blazed Trail. New York: Grossett & Dunlap, 1902.

The Riverman. New York: Grossett & Dunlap, 1908.

Histories

Butterfield, George E. Bay County Past and Present. Bay City, Mich.: Bay City Board of Education, 1918, and revised Centennial Edition, 1957.

History of Bay County, Michigan with illustrations and biographical sketches of some of its prominent men and pioneers. Chicago, Il; H. R. Page & Co 1883.

Indian and Pioneer History of the Saginaw Valley. East Saginaw, Mich.; Thomas Galatian, 1866.

Periodicals, Journals and Pamphlets

James Cloyd Bowman, "The Paul Bunyan Yarns," Michigan History Magazine,1941: 26-27.

Richard M. Dorson, "Folklore and Fake Lore," American Mercury 70 (1950):335-43.

Fred Dustin, "Saginaw County as a Center of Aboriginal Population." Michigan Historical Collections. Lansing: Michigan Historical Society, 1915.

Mary Jane Hennigar, "The First Paul Bunyan Story in Print," Journal of Forest History, October, 1986: 175-181.

Jeremy Kilar, "A Comparative Study of Lumber Barons as Community Leaders in Saginaw, Muskegon and Bay City," Michigan History, July/August, 1990: 35-42.

William B. Laughead, "Introducing Mr. Paul Bunyan of Westwood, Cal.", Red River Lumber Co., Minnesota, 1914, and subsequent editions (titles vary), including 1916-1922, "The Marvelous Exploits of Paul Bunyan," and 1922-1940, "Paul Bunyan and His Blue Ox.")

Elwood R. Maunder, "An Interview with James Stevens: The Making of a Folklorist," Forest History, Winter, 1964: 2-19.

Academic Papers and Reports

Fowke, Edith. "In Defense of Paul Bunyan," paper presented at the American Folklore Society meeting in Portland, Oregon, October 31, 1974. Published in New York Folklore, Summer, 1979.43-51..

Special Collections

Hotchkiss, George W. George W. Hotchkiss (1831 -1926) Papers, 1857-1927. Michigan Historical Collections of the University of Michigan, Ann Arbor.

Unpublished Manuscripts

Hotchkiss, Everitt S. "Reminiscences," Unpublished autobiography, typescript, Michigan Historical Collections of the University of Michigan, Ann Arbor.

Hotchkiss, George W. "Fifteen Years in Michigan," one chapter of autobiography, typescript, Michigan Historical Collections of the University of Michigan, Ann Arbor.

Selected Annotated Bibliography
on the Source and Authenticity
of the Paul Bunyan Legends

Ames, Carlton C. "Paul Bunyan: Myth or Hoax?" Minnesota History, 1940.

Botkin, Ben. Paul Bunyan. In: A Treasury of American Folklore, New York: Crown Publishers, 1944.

Bowman, James Cloyd. "The Paul Bunyan Yarns." Michigan History Magazine, 1941.

Charters, W.W. "Paul Bunyan in 1910." Journal of American Folklore, 1944. The author claims that the first written account of Paul Bunyan appeared in 1910.

Chase, Stuart. "Paul Bunyan." New Republic, 1925. James Stevens' Paul Bunyan is reviewed.

Davis, M.L. "Tall Tales; James Stevens of Paul Bunyan Fame." Sunset, May, 1929.

Dobie, J. Frank. "Paul Bunyan. Nation, 1925. Criticism of Stevens' and Shepard's books.

Dorson, Richard M. "America's Comic Demigod." American Scholar, 1941. Criticism of the Bunyan legends, called "fakelore" by this observer.

Felton, Harold V., ed. Legends of Paul Bunyan. New York: Alfred A. Knopf, 1947. 418 pp., illus., bibl. Including a comprehensive bibliography of Bunyan literature and other related works such as music, drama, painting and sculpture.

Halpert, Herbert. "A Note on Haney's Bibliography of Paul Bunyan." Journal of American Folklore, 1943.

Haney, Gladys J. "Paul Bunyan Represented in Art: A Bibliography." Journal of American Folklore, Vol. 55, 1942.

——— "Paul Bunyan Twenty Five Years After," Journal of American Folklore, Vol. 55, 1942. Comprehensive bibliography of all Bunyan material in the first 25 years after the original tales were printed.

Hartshorn, Mellor. Paul Bunyan: A Study in Folk Literature. Los Angeles, CA: Occidental College, 1934. 218 pp. Master's thesis with bibliography.

Hoffman, Daniel. Paul Bunyan: Last of the Frontier Demigods. 1966. Temple University Press. A defender of Paul Bunyan comes to the fore.

Hopkins, Bert. "Paul Bunyan, Only True American Myth." The Wisconsin Magazine, Vol. 1, 1933.

Laughead, W. B. The Marvelous Exploits of Paul Bunyan. In: In Our Times, Source Readers in American History No. 5. New York: The Macmillan Co., 1927.

———Paul Bunyan and His Big Blue Ox. Westwood, California: Red River Lumber Co., 1940, 40 pp. Part of the series of classic advertising brochures which spread the Bunyan tales.

Littell, Robert. "Paul Bunyan." New Republic, 1925. Esther Shepard's book is reviewed.

Malloch, Douglas. "Paul Bunyan." The American Lumberman, Chicago, IL, 1914. Poem jointly composed by Malloch and James MacGillivray which launched national attention to Paul Bunyan.

MacKaye, Percy. "A Homer of the Logging Camp." Bookman, 1925. Stevens' and Shepard's books are reviewed.

Owen, Ray S. "Paul Bunyan." Encyclopedia Brittanica, 14th Edition, 1929.

—"The Paul Bunyan Tales." Minnesota History, Vol. 21, 1940.

Pound, Louise. "Nebraska Strong Men." SFQ, Vol. 7, 1943. Paul Bunyan literature is reviewed.

Red River Lumber Co. "The Marvelous Exploits of Paul Bunyan. Minneapolis, Minnesota: 1922. 25 pp., illustrated. Lumber company advertising which was mailed nationwide and heightened public awareness about Paul Bunyan.

Rourke, Constance. American Humor. New York: Harcourt, Brace and Co., 1931. (pp. 233)

—"The Making of an Epic.. Saturday Review of Literature, 1925. Stevens' and Shepard's books are reviewed.
—"Paul Bunyan—Lumberjack." New Republic, 1920.

Shephard, Esther. Paul Bunyan. New York: Harcourt, Brace and Co., 1924. Rep. 1941. 233 pp., illus. First book on Paul Bunyan, comprised of stories collected from the Northwest.

Stevens, James. "The Black Duck Dinner. American Mercury, 1924. The fanciful story which began the growth of new literature about Paul Bunyan.

—Paul Bunyan. New York: Alfred A. Knopf, 1925. 245 pp., illus. Stevens' first book which became the alltime bestseller on Bunyan.

—"Paul Bunyan Stories." Saturday Review of Literature, 1926. Replying to Bates' criticism of his book.

—The Saginaw Paul Bunyan. New York: Alfred A. Knopf, 1932. 261 pp. Woodcuts by Richard Bennett. More Bunyan tales; written in response to criticism after Stevens spent a year in Michigan researching the tales, proclaiming Saginaw Country as the home of Bunyan. (Reprinted in 1987 by Wayne State University Press, Detroit, Michigan.)

Stewart, K. Bernice, and Watt, Homer A. "Legends of Paul Bunyan, Lumberjack." Transactions of the Wisconsin Academy of Sciences, Arts and Letters, 1916. Recounting tall tales by lumbermen.

Stokes, Richard L. "Review of Paul Bunyan by R.L. Stokes." Nation, 1933.

Tabor, Edward O., and Thompson, Stith. "Paul Bunyan in 1910." Journal of American Folklore, 1946.

Turney, Ida V. A New Literary Type, With Special References to the Tales of Paul Bunyan. Ph.D. Thesis—University of Oregon.

Van Doren, Carl. The American Novel: 1789-1939. New York: The Macmillan Co., 1940.

Watt, Homer A. The Rise of Realism. Louis Wann, ed. New York: The Macmillan Co., 1933. Discussion of Paul Bunyan's status in American folklore.

Index

APPENDIX A

An American Legendary Hero

(James Stevens on the Paul Bunyan legend)

...Superficially the legends and the hero seems to indicate no more than the plain American's talent for the humor of exaggeration. But they go deeper than that.

The loggers themselves are unconscious of having made him a demi-god. But their conception of Bunyan, nevertheless, is their recognition of the sublime. While they regard him as one of themselves, they place him above their own appetites and weaknesses.

The condition of the roving laborers made it quite natural for them to give their hero attributes of divinity. Feeling barred from Christian heaven by their own life, and scorned by the godly of the villages, they were compelled to devise their own consolations and dreams of a richer life.

Consider for a moment a typical logger in a period of hard times. His earnings squandered, he is driven by a righteous constable from the town where they were spent. He tramps slowly down the railroad track, counting the ties. As he increases the miles behind him weariness and hunger torment his flesh. There are farmhouses across the fields, but they are the abodes of virtue and thrift; every window seems a hostile eye. At dusk, however, the logger yields, with great self-loathing, and knocks on a kitchen door. More humiliating than a beating is the silent contempt with which a handout is given him. He trudges through the fields, a hulking, shambling Shame. At a haystack he sprawls out and prepares to eat. What use is he now, he thinks, when no one wants his labor? What good now are the prideful muscles that made physical exultation of toil in the woods? He knows that when he gets another stake he will "blow it" as before. He has sinned so much that no repentance could save him from Hell. He is just a poor, weak, miserable critter, that's all. Why was he born? Thus he ruminates as he chews greedily on crusts of bread and stares at the distant pines, which in the starlight seem like rough black blankets thrown over the hills. The logger thinks mournfully of the closed camps. And now as his hunger lessens he seeks some sustenance of consolation and hope for his soul. Memories of the brighter side of camp-life come to him, memories of the pleasures of feasting, of companionship, stories and songs. And of course he remembers Paul Bunyan. He muses... "Say, if they only' was a Paul Bunyan, now" he murmurs. He grins over the fancy and seeks more cheer from it. He pictures Paul Bunyan and the blue ox journeying over the hills, colossal but obscure figures in the faint light. Ere they disappear the good and mighty Bunyan turns, his beard moves in a magnificent smile, and he beckons to the unfortunate with a grand flourish... There is a water-tank on up the track and the logger starts for it with a lively step when he hears the muffled whistle of a train. He chuckles. "Maybe ol' Bunyan has got a camp over the hump". No longer is he a lonely and despairing man. Paul Bunyan is his captain, the commander of his soul. The old hero has lived over half a century now, and he will endure as long as there is a refuge for primitive innocence and spontaneity in the deep woods.

APPENDIX B

THE BLAZED TRAIL, by Stewart Edward White (1873-1946)

Published by Grossett & Dunlap, New York, 1902
Chapter XXVI

A lumbering town after the drive is a fearful thing. Men just off the river draw a deep breath, and plunge into the wildest reactionary dissipations. In droves they invade the cities, — wild, picturesque, lawless. As long as the money lasts, they blow it in.

"Hot money!" is the cry. "She's burn holes in all my pockets already!"

The saloons are full, the gambling houses overflow, all the places of amusement or crime run full blast. A chip rests lightly on everyone's shoulder. Fights are as common as raspberries in August. Often one of these formidable men, his muscles toughened and quickened by the active, strenuous river work, will set out to "take the town apart." For a time he leaves rack and ruin, black eyes and broken teeth behind him, until he meets a more redoubtable "knocker" and is pounded and kicked into unconsciousness. Organized gangs go from house to house forcing the peaceful inmates to drink from their bottles. Others take possession of certain sections of the street and resist a' l'outrance the attempts of others to pass. Inoffensive citizens are stood on their heads, or shaken upside down until the contents of their pockets rattle on the street. Parenthetically, these contents are invariably returned to their owners. The riverman's object is fun, not robbery.

And if rip-roaring, swashbuckling, drunken glory is what he is after, he gets it. The only trouble is, that a whole winter's hard work goes in two or three weeks. The only redeeming feature is, that he is never, in or out of his cups, afraid of anything that walks the earth.

A man comes out of the woods or off the drive with two or three hundred dollars, which he is only too anxious to throw away by the double handful. It follows naturally that a crew of sharpers are on hand to find out who gets it. They are a hard lot. Bold, unprincipled men, they too are afraid of nothing; not even a drunken lumber-jack, which is one of the dangerous wild animals of the American fauna. Their business is to relieve the man of his money as soon as possible. They are experts at their business.

The towns of Bay City and Saginaw alone in 1878 supported over fourteen hundred tough characters. Block after block was devoted entirely to saloons. In a radius of three hundred feet from the famous old Catacombs could be numbered forty saloons, where drinks were sold by from three to ten "pretty waiter girls." When the boys struck town, the proprietors and waitresses stood in their doorways to welcome them.

"Why, Jack!" one would cry, "when did you drift in? Tickled to death to see you! Come in an' have a drink. That your chum? Come in, old man, and have a drink. Never mind the pay; that's all right."

And after the first drink, Jack, of course, had to treat, and then the chum.

Or if Jack resisted temptation and walked resolutely on, one of the girls would remark audibly to another.

"He ain't no lumber-jack! You can see that easy 'nuff! He's jest off th' hay-trail!"

Ten to one that brought him, for the woodsman is above all things proud and jealous of his craft.

In the center of this whirlpool of iniquity stood the Catacombs as the hub from which lesser spokes in the wheel radiated. Any old logger of the Saginaw Valley can tell you of the Catacombs, just as any old logger of any other valley will tell you of the "Pen," the "White Row," the "Water Streets" of Alpena, Port Huron, Ludington, Muskegon, and a dozen other lumber towns.

The Catacombs was a three-story building. In the basement were vile, ill-smelling, ill-lighted dens, small, isolated, dangerous. The shanty boy with a small stake, far gone in drunkenness, there tasted the last drop of wickedness, and thence was flung unconscious and penniless on the streets. A trap-door directly into the river accommodated those who were inconsiderate enough to succumb under rough treatment.

The second story was given over to drinking. Polly Dickson there reigned supreme, an anomaly. She was as pretty and fresh and pure-looking as a child; and at the same time was one of the most ruthless and unscrupulous of the gang. She could at will exercise a fascination the more terrible in that it appealed at once to her victim's nobler instincts of reverence, his capacity for what might be called aesthetic fascination, as well as his passions. When she finally held him, she crushed him as calmly as she would a fly.

Four bars supplied the drinkables. Dozens of "pretty waiter girls" served the customers. A force of professional fighters was maintained by the establishment to preserve that degree of peace which should look to the preservation of mirrors and glassware.

The third story contained a dance hall and a theater. The character of both would better be left to the imagination.

Night after night during the season, this den ran at top-steam.

By midnight, when the orgy was at its height, the windows brilliantly illuminated, the various bursts of music, laughing, cursing, singing, shouting, fighting, breaking in turn or all together from its open windows, it was, as Jackson Hines once expressed it to me, like hell let out for noon.

The respectable elements of the towns were powerless. They could not control the elections. Their police would only have risked total annihilation by attempting a raid. At the first sign of trouble they walked straightly in the paths of their own affairs, awaiting the time soon to come when, his take "blown-in," the last bitter dregs of pleasure gulped down, the shanty boy would again start for the woods.

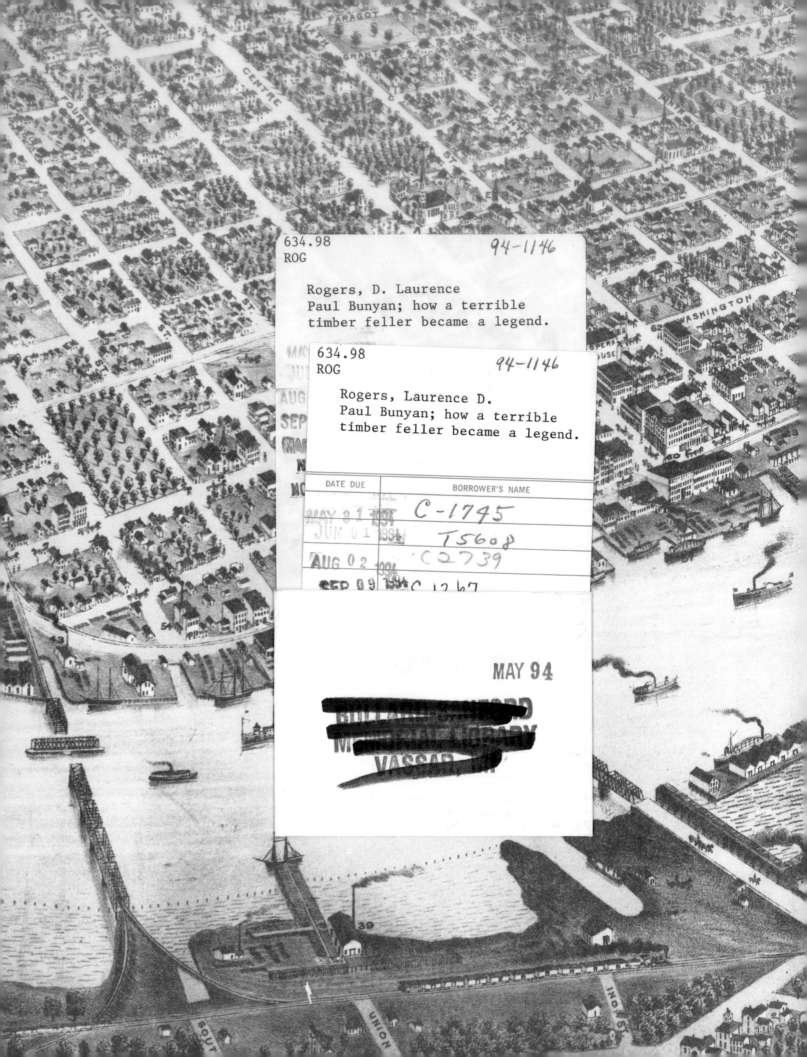